C000118185

1 MONTH OF
FREE
READING

at
www.ForgottenBooks.com

By purchasing this book you are
eligible for one month membership to
ForgottenBooks.com, giving you
unlimited access to our entire
collection of over 1,000,000 titles via
our web site and mobile apps.

To claim your free month visit:

www.forgottenbooks.com/free884567

* Offer is valid for 45 days from date of purchase. Terms and conditions apply.

ISBN 978-0-266-75249-3
PIBN 10884567

This book is a reproduction of an important historical work. Forgotten Books uses
state-of-the-art technology to digitally reconstruct the work, preserving the original format
whilst repairing imperfections present in the aged copy. In rare cases, an imperfection in
the original, such as a blemish or missing page, may be replicated in our edition. We do,
however, repair the vast majority of imperfections successfully; any imperfections that
remain are intentionally left to preserve the state of such historical works.

Forgotten Books is a registered trademark of FB &c Ltd.
Copyright © 2018 FB &c Ltd.
FB &c Ltd, Dalton House, 60 Windsor Avenue, London, SW19 2RR.
Company number 08720141. Registered in England and Wales.

For support please visit www.forgottenbooks.com

THE RELIGIOUS DEVELOPMENT

OF

POQUONOCK AND RAINBOW

A THESIS

Submitted to the Faculty

of the

HARTFORD SCHOOL OF RELIGIOUS EDUCATION
HARTFORD SEMINARY FOUNDATION

In candidacy for the degree of

MASTER OF ART

DEPARTMENT OF EDUCATION

CHARLOTTE PHELPS KENDRICK

May 27, 1936

BR
555
C9
W5

Charlotte Phelps Kendrick
Windsor, Connecticut

PREFACE

The Poquonock Community (Congregational Incorporated) Church will celebrate its one hundredth anniversary in 1941. It is the purpose of this paper to prepare an historical source book which will be useful in preparing a pageant to be given during the coming church celebration.

Four things were kept in mind when writing the paper: first, in order to understand fully the development of the present Community Church one must understand the early religious life in the community. Second the development of one religious group is influenced by the social, religious, educational and economic conditions of the surrounding communities as well as by conditions in its own community. Third, the development of one religious group cannot be fully appreciated without studying the other religious groups in the community. Fourth, the material should be as accurate as possible and written in an unbiased manner.

The material for the paper was gathered mainly from papers, letters, notebooks and diaries found in various attics. The writer realizes that the writing of this paper would have been impossible without the cooperation of the people in the community who have given permission to quote from letters, to search in attics and to borrow valued scrapbooks and papers.

Former inhabitants and their descendants, librarians and ministers, have given valuable assistance.

INTRODUCTION
Search for Freedom

During the early part of the seventeenth century England was overcast by the thick gathering cloud of civil and religious persecution. James the First ruled as an absolute monarch. He said of the Puritans, one group of dissenters, "I will make them conform or I will harry them out of the land."

His son, Charles the First, ascended the throne in 1625.

"The king's philosophy was fittingly expressed in his own words, which he later uttered as he stood upon the scaffold prepared for death, 'Their (the people's) liberty and freedom consists in having government, ... it is not in their having a share in the government, that is nothing pertaining to them'.[1]

Everyone was compelled by law to worship in the established church of which the King claimed to be the head. Those who refused to obey the decrees of the church were crushed with despotic cruelty.

The dissenters may be divided into three main groups: (1) Those who still clung to the church in hopes of reforming it. They were called Puritans. (2) Those who dissented because they saw no hope of reform. The Pilgrims belonged to this group. (3) Those who believed the established church was not in conformity with the New Testament.

"The clergy of the Church of England were at a difference in regard to wearing what John Fox called 'Mathematical caps with four corners', and 'theatrical dresses', and 'Popish insignia'. A royal decree published in March 1564 made it imperative upon all ministers of the Gospel to wear the regulation vestments when officiating at Divine service. Dissent from this decree by many ministers became so strenuous that the Archbishop told the Queen in regard to the dissenters, 'These precise folks would offer their goods, and their bodies, to prison rather than relent.' Then the dissenters were first called Puritans, as 'men that did profess a greater purity in the worship of God, and a greater detestation of the ceremonies and corruptions of Rome, than the rest of their brethren'.

---

[1] Howard, Daniel, A New History of Old Windsor, Conn., page 12, Windsor Locks, Conn., The Journal Press, 1935.

"The Puritan made himself conspicuous by resisting the impositions of the rubric as to the use of the cross in baptism, the ring in marriage, and the kneeling posture at the communion. He refused to join in religious services under the guidance of the minister wearing a surplice or other vestments of the Church of England. He could say:
'I am no quaker not at all to sweare,
Nor papist to sweare east and mean a west,
But am a protestant and will declare
What I can nott and what I can protest.
Paul had a cloake and bookes and parchment too,
But that he wore a Surplice I'll not sweare,
Nor that his parchments did his orders show,
Or in his bookes there was a common prayer'."[1]

America, for many years, had been known as a land for exploration and fur trade. It came now to be regarded by many as a place not only where they might enjoy civil and religious freedom, but also where they might establish their own form of government. They were opposed to many social and political customs of the day as well as to the practices of the established Church.

Among the people who came to America were a group of Puritans from the southern part of England. Before leaving England on the "Mary and John" they organized themselves into a church.

The members of the Church lived at Dorchester, Massachusetts for five years. They were not entirely satisfied as they were of a more democratic nature than their neighbors.

"The group of settlements around the Massachusetts Bay was dominated by clergymen and Officials of Aristocratic tendencies. Their governor, John Winthrop declared, 'The best part (of the people) is always the least, and of that best part the wiser part is always the lesser'. The Rev. John Cotton put it more bluntly when he said, 'Never did God ordain democracy for the government of the church or people'."[1]

The Dorchester group then turned to Connecticut as a place where they hoped to find even more freedom.[2] By April 1636 almost all of the Dorchester Church and their pastor Rev. Mr. Warham had left old Dorchester, Massachusetts for their new home in Connecticut.

---

[1] Bliss, William Root, Side Glimpses From the Colonial Meeting-House, pages 32-34, Boston, Massachusetts, Houghton, Mifflin & Company, 1894.

[1] Howard, Daniel, A New History of Old Windsor, Connecticut, page 13, Windsor Locks, Connecticut, The Journal Press, 1935.

[2] Note: For an account of other early settlers of Connecticut see Stiles, Henry R., The History of Ancient Windsor, Connecticut, pages 1-29, 348 Broadway, New York, N. Y., Charles B. Norton, 1859.

CHAPTER I

EARLY RELIGIOUS LIFE

A. Settlement of Windsor

The fertile fields of the Connecticut River proved not only pleasing to the Dorchester group but to others as well. One of the first things the settlers had to do was to come to terms with the already settled Plymouth Group and the new group known as the Lords and Ladies. All three groups claimed their right of settlement. The land was divided and the Lords and Ladies and the Dorchester group were soon busy making their new homes.

> "Until they could prepare or procure the material for better homes they were obliged to live in rude shelters consisting of cellar-like rooms excavated in the side of the rising ground along the edge of the meadow or the river bank. The rear end and the two sides of each dug-out were simply of the earth itself, partly that which had been undisturbed and partly that which had been taken out of the excavation. The roof of beams and poles was thatched with wild grass. They probably placed hewn planks upon the floor, but we have no record to prove this. The front end was also without doubt protected by hewn boards, or stakes. In the following year, 1637, danger from the Pequot Indians led all the settlers to abandon their dug-outs on the 'sandy bank' and come together on and around the area now known as the Palisado Green. Their new homes were at once enclosed with a strong palisado."[1]

B. Government of Windsor

Before the settlers came to Connecticut they had agreed to remain under the authority of the Massachusetts Government. The general court of Massachusetts set up a commission of eight members with Roger Ludlow at their head to govern the river settlement for the year 1636. The first meeting was held at Newtown (Hartford) on April 26, 1638. It was called a corte (court). Roger Ludlow was the first President. Henry Wolcott was appointed constable for Dorchester. The court made laws to meet the physical, social and spiritual needs of the people. The next year the commission was called the General Court. The names of the River Towns had been changed from Newtown to Hartford, Dorchester[1] to Windsor[2] and Watertown to Wethersfield.

---

[1] Howard, Daniel, A New History of Old Windsor, Connecticut, page 14, Windsor Locks, Connecticut, The Journal Press, 1935.

[1] Dorchester was named in honor of the Rev. Mr. White of Dorchester, England. See Stiles, Henry R, The History of Ancient Windsor, Conn., pages 5, 6, 7, 348 Broadway, New York, N. Y., Charles B. Norton, 1859.

[2] Windsor may have been named in honor of the royal palace of England's sovereigns. See Stiles, Henry R, Ibid.

After many months of planning a new constitution was drafted for Connecticut. It shows not only English and Dutch influence but originality as well. Six of the most important principles of this constitution were the following:

"All the authority of government comes directly from the people.

"The form of government shall consist of a governor, a body of magistrates, and deputies or representatives chosen by the towns.

"There shall be no taxation without representation.

"The number of men that the towns shall choose to make their laws shall be in proportion to the population of the towns.

"All freemen who take an oath to be faithful to the state shall have the right to vote.

"New towns may join the three original towns and live under the same government.

"This first constitution became the model for all constitutions that have since been adopted in America. Many changes and additions have been made to it in Connecticut, while other states have changed it to suit themselves but everywhere in the United States and in other republics the teachings of Thomas Hooker[1] and Roger Ludlow have shown men how to form good governments."[2]

"This constitution is regarded as the first in the history of the world that created a new government and prescribed how the people who created it and were to live under it should be governed."[3]

C. *Early Church Life in Windsor*

1. *Church officers.* The early churches were highly organized. Each church had a pastor, teacher, one or more ruling elders, and deacons. Another officer which should be mentioned is the tythingman, although he was not elected by the church.

The duties of the church officers[1] were clearly defined. The pastor was to exhort, persuade and sympathize with his people. The teacher was to explain and defend the doctrines of Christianity. The ruling elder who was also ordained, was to assist in the government of the church, have charge of the discipline and assist in every service except the preaching and the sacraments. Occasionally he delivered the weekday lecture.

---

[1] Thomas Hooker: At the session of the General Court at Hartford, Conn., May 31, 1638 he preached his famous sermon "The Fundamental Principles of Civil Government". The sermon put forth the principles which were drafted later into the Constitution.

[2] Howard, Daniel, A New History of Old Windsor, Conn., page 32, Windsor Locks, Conn., The Journal Press, 1935.

[3] Howard, Daniel, A New History of Old Windsor, Conn., page 32, Windsor Locks, Conn., The Journal Press, 1935.

[1] Duties were based on the following Bible passages: Romans 12:7, I Corinthians 12:28, I Timothy 5:17 and Ephesians 4:11.

The tythingman was a parish officer. He was elected annually to preserve good order in the meeting-house and to prevent any violations of the many laws which were designed to make the Sabbath a day given over wholly to religious matters.

One of his tasks was to keep the children[2] quiet during the church service. Occasionally he reminded a nodding adult that divine service was going on. He also listened for the sound of an approaching carriage. If the driver was unable to give a good reason for traveling on the sabboth he was arrested.

2. *Financial support of the minister.* There is a very interesting law which was made September 5, 1644.

> "Every man should set down voluntarily what he was willing to give for ministerial support. If any man should refuse to pay, he was to be rated by the authorities, who should exercise the same procedure to force payment as for other debts."[1]

The Code of 1650 required all to contribute to the support of the church. Taxes or rates for the support of the ministry were to be made and collected in the same manner as rates for the town.

3. *Church membership.* Every church was united in a covenant. The members solemnly renewed their obligations to the Lord and to each other. They did this by recommendation of the court, on days of public humiliation and at times of disaster.

The candidate for church membership was examined by the officers of the church. At a later date the examination was held before the church. Still later the men were examined orally and the women in written form.

One of the early church controversies was over the question of church membership.

At first church membership was limited to those who professed having had a religious experience but they also held that children shared in their parents' covenanting and were therefore truly members of the church. Baptism to children was granted only to those who had at least one parent a member of the church. Several questions arose—one was in regard to parents who wanted their children to belong to the church and yet could not point to any personal religious experience. The next question was is a person a church member whose parents were members and yet who were

---

[2] Children did not sit with their parents. Judging from other church records unruly boys caused a great deal of trouble.
[1] Colonial Record of Connecticut, Vol. I, p. 112, Hartford, Connecticut, Case, Lockwood & Brainard Company.

not considered regenerated. A double classification of members was introduced—full members and then those (not considered regenerated) who could not vote on church government or receive the Lord's Supper. The opponents of the system nicknamed it the Half-Way Covenant. The Windsor Church was the first church to adopt the Half-Way Covenant.

4. *Church services.* The people were called to worship by the beating of a drum, a place having been built on the roof for the sexton to stand while beating the drum.

Everyone in town came, many of them walking a long distance and having a river to cross. If one stayed home from service without a good reason he was fined five shillings.

A definite place was assigned for everyone. Rules and regulations for seating were made until it was assumed to be "a dignifying of the meeting-house".

Rules for seating or "dignifying of the meeting-house" were not the same in all towns. The factors which influenced the decision were about the same being: (1) Ancestry, (2) Position in town, (3) Pious living, (4) Estate, (5) Age, (6) Special service rendered to the town. In Windsor as in other places provision was made for people who were hard of hearing. They were allowed to sit on the pulpit stairs, or near by.

The church was unlighted, in fact evening meetings were not thought of until singing schools were started. The early settlers were opposed to stoves or fireplaces in the meeting-house. In winter the meeting-house was a cold place.

"It may be said that the congregation sat shivering on the brink of perdition, if the icy temperature of the house and the terrible doctrines of the sermon are to be taken together."[1]

We do not know exactly what the early services were like. Printed programs and order of services were unknown then.

The Puritans were revolting against many outward forms of the Church of England. Their service was, therefore, very simple consisting of Prayer, Reading the Scripture, Psalm Singing and the Sermon.

There were many versions of the Psalms. One of the first versions used, was that of Sternhold and Hopkins. This was printed at the end of their Bibles. The New England Psalm Book was used for many years. It was printed as early as 1640.

---

[1] Bliss, William Root, Side Glimpses From the Colonial Meeting-House, p. 49, Boston, Mass., Houghton, Mifflin & Co., 1894.

4

The sermons were long but that did not prevent the people from having a service in the afternoon. The church was sometimes catechised during the intermission of public worship. The Sabbath was a day given over entirely to religious thought.

The weekday lecture also was an important service. Almost everyone was in the center of town on that day.

Fast days were also kept by the people. Thanksgiving Day was the only religious holiday. Christmas and Easter were considered Papal.

D. *Rules and Laws Concerning Religious Education*

The Puritan had little need for books outside of the Bible as it contained, to his way of thinking, the authoritative rules for life.

The Bible used by the Puritans was the Geneva Bible. This version (1560) "Attained its great popularity and fame by its prologues and marginal notes".[1] Many of the notes are anti-papal, therefore were very well liked by over-jealous Reformers. Calvin was then the ruling spirit. The notes express his belief concerning theological, ecclesiastical, political and social problems.

One of the reasons for the King James Version of the Bible was that the King disliked the political ideas expressed in the marginal notes. For many years after the publication of the King James Version the Geneva Bible was the most popular one in New England.

There was a religious motive back of the Puritan's plan for education for religion to the Puritan permeated all of life.

We read in the code of 1650 under schools:

"It being one chiefe project of that old deluder Satan, to keepe men from the knowledge of the Scriptures, as in former times, keeping them in an unknowne tongue, so in these latter times, by persuading them from the use of Tongues, so that at least, the true sence and meaning of the originall might bee clouded with false glasses of saint seeming deceivers and that Learning may not bee buried in the Grave of our Forefathers, in church and Common wealth, the Lord assisting our indeavors, It is therefore ordered by this Courte and Authority thereof, That every Towneshipp within this jurissdiction after the Lord hath increased them to the number of fifty househoulders, shall then forthwith appoint one within theire towne to teach all such children as shall resorte to him, to write and read, whose wages shall bee paid either by the parents or masters of such children,

---

[1] Jackson, Samuel Macauley, The New Schaff-Herzog Encyclopedia Volume II, page 158, Bibles, Annotated and Bible Summaries, New York, N. Y., Funk and Wagnalls Company, 1908.

5

or by the Inhabitants in generale, by way of supplye, as the maior parte of those who order the prudentialls of the town shall appointe, provided, that those who send theire children bee not oppressed by more than they can have them taught for in other townes."[1]

Provision was also made for instruction in the homes of not only children but servants also for in the code of 1650 in the section under children we read:

"Forasmuch as the good Education of children is of singular behoofe and benefitt to any common wealth, and whereas many parents and masters are too indulgent and negligent of theire duty in that kinde, It is therefore ordered by this courte and the authority thereof, that the selectmen of every towne in the severall precincts and quarters where they dwell, shall have a vigilant eye over theire brethren and neighbours, to see, first, that none of them shall suffer so much barbarisme in theire familyes, as not to endeavor to teach by themselves or others, theire children and Apprentices so much Learning, as may enable them perfectly to read the Inglish tongue, and knowledge of the capitall Laws, upon penalty of twenty shillings for each neglect therein; also, that all Masters of familyes doe once a week, at least, catechise theire children and servants, in the grounds and principles of religion; and if any bee unable to doe so much, that then at the least they procure such children or Apprentices to learne some shorte orthodox catechisme without booke, that they may bee able to answer to the questions that shall bee propounded to them out of such Catechismes by theire parents, or masters, or any of the Selectmen, when they shall call them to a tryall of what they have learned in this kinde. And further, that all parents and Masters doe breed and bring up their children and Apprentices in some honest lawfull calling, labor or employment, either in husbandry or some other trade proffitable for themselves and the common weath, if they will not nor cannot traine them up in Learning, to fitt them for higher employments; And if any of the selectmen after Adomition by them given to such Masters of familyes, shall finde them still neglectfull, of theire duty, in the perticulars aforementioned, whereby Children and Servants become rude, stubborne and unruly, the said selectment with the helpe of two Magistrates shall take such Children or Apprentices from them, and place them with some masters for yeares,—boys till they come to twenty-one and girles to eighteen yeares of age compleat which will more strictly looke unto and force them to submitt unto government, according to the rules of this order, if faire meanes and former instructions they will not bee drawne into it."[1]

[1] Hoadley, C. J., and Trumbull, J. Hammond, Colonial Records of Connecticut, Vol. I., pages 554, 555, Hartford, Connecticut, Case, Lockwood & Brainard Company.
[1] Hoadley, C. J., and Trumbull, J. Hammond, Colonial Records of Connecticut, Vol. I, page 520, 521, Hartford, Conn, Case, Lockwood & Brainard Company.

Apparently the rules made in 1650 were not sufficient to foster religious instruction for all. At a court held in Hartford, May 11, 1676 the following law was passed:

"Wheras reading the scripture Catechizing the children and daily prayer with giving of thanks is part of God's worship and the homage due him to be attended conscientiously by every Christian family to distinguish them from the heathen who call not upon God, and the neglect of it a great sin, provoking God to pour forth wrath on such families or persons, for redress thereof, where any such neglect may be found, this court do solemnly recommend it to the ministry in all places, to look into the state of such families, convince them of and instruct them in their duty, and by all due means encourage them that none be found among us utterly ignorant and profane."[1]

Further on we read the provision made for the carrying out of the law.

"But if any heads or governors of such families shall be obstinate and refractory and will not be reformed, that the grand jury present such persons to the county court to be fined or punished or bound to good behavior, according to the demerits of the case."[2]

In 1680 we find reference to religious instruction for boys and girls on the Sabbath. The general court ordered

"For the better preservation and propagation of religion to posterity, it is ordered by this court that it be recommended to the ministry of this colony to catechise the youth in their respective places that are under twenty years of age, in the assembly of Divines Catechism, or some other orthodox catechism on the Sabbath days."[3]

Although schools were becoming more common there were still many people who were unable to read. The court realized this fact and felt that more drastic measures must be taken in order to have Education more prevalent.

On May 13, 1690 the court passed a law, with provision for enforcement, which they hoped would correct the lack of knowledge of reading among many.

It reads as follows:

"This Court, observing that, not withstanding the former orders made for the erudition of children and servants, there are many persons unable to read the Holy Word of God, or the good laws of the Colony, which evil, that it grow no further upon their

---

[1] Hoadley, C. J., and Trumbull, J. Hammond, Colonial Records of Connecticut, page 281, Vol. II., Hartford, Conn., Case, Lockwood & Brainard Company.
[2] Ibid, Vol. II, Page 281.
[3] Ibid, Vol. III, pages 147-148.

Majesties subjects here, it is hereby ordered that all parents and masters shall cause their respective children and servants, as they are capable to be taught to read distinctly the English tongue and that the grand jurymen in each town do once in the year at least visit each family they suspect to neglect this order."[1]

E. Qualifications of a Freeman

1. *Rules and regulations.* We have mentioned before that one reason for the Dorchester group leaving Massachusetts was to settle in a place where they could have more freedom. We are not surprised then to find the requirements for being admitted a freeman less exacting than in Massachusetts.

The Puritan has been both idealized and severely criticized. To some he is accredited with almost every virtue. By some people he is called a "lover of freedom" to others he is considered one of the most bigoted of men.

The writer feels that under the circumstances it is best to let the records speak for themselves.

"At the first session of the General Assembly under the Charter October 9, 1662 it was ordered that those who desired to be admitted freeman should obtain a certificate from a majority of the Townsmen, certifying that they are persons of civil, peaceable and honest conservation and that they have attained to the age of twenty-one years, and have £20 estate (besides their rent Poll), in the list of Estate, and such certificate shall be presented to the court authorized to admit freeman. Provision was made at the same time for the disfranchisement of such as were convicted of scandalous offences."[1]

During the administration of Cromwell, the colonists had been allowed to manage their own affairs with little interference. When Charles the Second ascended the throne he inquired into the administration of the Colonial Government.

At the General Assembly held in Hartford, April 20, 1668 the colonists assured the King's Commissioners that they knew of no one who had been troubled by them because of differences of belief so long as they had not disturbed others.

2. *Laws concerning religion.* We turn to the Colonial and Town Records to find many rules and regulations concerning religious matters.

---

[1] Hoadley, C. J., and Trumbull, J. Hammond, Colonial Records of Connecticut, Vol. IV. page 30, Hartford, Conn., Case, Lockwood & Brainard Company.
[1] Stiles, Henry R, The History of Ancient Windsor, Connecticut, pages 56, 57, 348 Broadway, New York, N. Y., Charles B. Norton, 1859.

We read:

"It is ordered by this Courte and decreed, that the Civill Authority heere established hath power and libberty to see the peace ordinances and rules of Christe bee observed in every Church according to his word, as allso to deale with any church member in a way of Civill (justice) not withstanding any Church relation, office or interest, so it bee done in a Civill and not in an Ecclesiasticall way; nor shall any church censure, degrade or depose any man from any Civill dignitye office or authority hee shall have in the Common wealth."[1]

The General Court on the first of December, 1642 decreed:

1. "Yf any man after legall conviction shall have or worship any other God but the Lord God, he shall be put to death. Deuteronomy 13:6, 17:2. Exodus 22:20."[2]

3. "Uf any prson shall blaspheme the name of God the Father, Son or Holy Gaste, wth direct, expres, prsumptuous or highhanded blasphemy, or shall curse God in the like manner he shall be put to death. Leviticus 24:15".[3]

3. *Laws concerning dress.* Regulation of dress was made soon for we read in the record of April 10, 1640,

"Not wthstanding the late Order Concerning the restraynt of excesse in apparrell, yet dievers prsons of severall ranks are obsearved still to exceede therein. It is therefore Ordered that the Constables of every Towne wthin these libertyes, shall obsearve and take notice of any prticular prson or prsons wthin their severall lymitts and all such as they judge to exceede their condition and ranks therein, they shall prsent and warne to appeare at the prticular Courte."[4]

4. *Methods of punishment.* Many people think immediately of punishment, stocks and whipping posts when the word Puritan or early settler is mentioned.

Let us turn to the town records. We read in the town payments of 1663 that William Buell charged for making a pair of stocks.

In February 1640

"Mr. Webster and Mr. Phelps are desired to consult wth the Elders of boath Plantations to prpare instructions agt the next

---

[1] Hoadley, C. J., and Trumbull, J. Hammond, Colonial Records of Connecticut, Vol. I, pages 524-525, Hartford, Conn., Case, Lockwood & Brainard Company.
[2] Ibid, Vol. I, Page 77.
[3] Ibid, Vol. I, page 77.
[4] Ibid, Vol. I, page 64. Particular Court: Twelve jurors dealt in civil actions, debts and tresspasses of over forty shillings in value, and with grave crimes and wrongs.

Court for the punisheing of the sin of lying wch begins to be practised by many prsons in this Comonweth."[1]

The next year we read September 9th, 1641:

"For the prventing and avoyding that foule and grasse sin of lying, yt is Ordered, that when any prson or prsons shall bee accused and proved guilty of that vice, yt shall be lawfull for the prticular Courte to adjudge and censure any such prty, ether by fyne or bodily correction according as they shall judge the nature of the fault to require, this to hold to the next court."[2]

The Code of 1650 made provision for the punishment of those who committed the crime of lying. Anyone over fourteen who lied was to be fined not more than twelve shillings or to stay in the stocks not over three hours. After the second offence he was to be fined twenty shillings or be whipped no more than twenty stripes upon the naked body. Provision was made for more harsh punishment if any one persisted in lying.

Profane swearing was punishable in a similiar way.

Whipping and placing in the stocks were generally performed upon a lecture day or training day. Whether or not seeing the results of doing wrong prevented wrong being done we do not know.

We have preserved in the Town Records several accounts of punisment in early Windsor.

"June 2, 1664. Mr. ___ ___ for his cursing at Windsor before the Train band last Monday is to pay to the public treasury 10 shillings."[1]

"In 1670 ___ ___ of Windsor was deposed from his office of Constable for swearing and drunkness."[2]

Branding was another method of punishment. A second offence was followed by a second branding, and severe whipping. If the crime was committed on the Sabbath one of the culprit's ears was cut off.

"September 1644 ___ ___ for his theft is adjudged to restore fourfold for what shall be proved before Captain Mason and Mr. Wolcott, and to be branded in the hand, the next training-day at Windsor."[3]

---

[1] Hoadley, C. J., and Trumbull, J. Hammond, Colonial Records of Connecticut, Vol. I, page 62, Hartford, Conn., Case, Lockwood & Brainard Company.
[2] Ibid, Vol. I, page 68.
[1] Stiles, Henry R, The History of Ancient Windsor, Connecticut, page 67, 348 Broadway, New York, N. Y., Charles B. Norton, 1859.
[2] Ibid, page 68.
[3] Ibid, page 69.

5. *Tobacco law.* One of the most interesting laws passed was the tobacco law.

In May 1647 the Court said:

"Forasmuch as it is observed that many abuses are crept in and committed by frequent taking of Tobacco, it is ordered by the authority of this Court, that no person under the age of twenty-one years, nor any other that hath not already accustomed himself to the use thereof, shall take any tobacco until he have brought a certificate, under the hand of some who are approved for knowledge and skill in physic, that it is useful for him, and also that he hath received a license from the Court for the same. And for the regulating those who either by their former taking it, have to their own apprehensions made it necessary to them, or upon due advice are persuaded to the use thereof, it is ordered that no man within this Colony, after the publication hereof, shall take it in the fields or woods, unless when they are on their travel, or journey of at least ten miles, or at the ordinary time of repast commonly called dinner, or if it be not then taken, yet not then above once in the day at most, and then not in company with anyone. Nor shall any inhabitant in any of the towns within this jurisdiction, take any tobacco in any house in the same town where he liveth, with and in the company of any more than one who useth and drinketh the same weed, with him at any time, under the penalty of six pence, in any of the particulars thereof, to be paid without gainsaying, upon conviction by the testimony of one witness that is without just exception before any one Magistrate."[1]

6. *Temperance.* About the same time a law was passed forbidding anyone to drink more than three pints at a time.

7. *Roger Ludlow and the Code of 1650.* A report of the early laws would be incomplete without due credit being given to Roger Ludlow of Windsor. The General Court in April 1646 assigned to him the task of drafting a body of laws for Connecticut.

Several years later (May 1650) these laws were established. They are generally spoken of as the Code of 1650 although sometimes called "Ludlow's Code". The laws were intended to provide for every need and situation of vital concern to the Colony. Many of the laws have been referred to especially in the section on religious education.

F. Decline in Puritanism

The period 1690 to about 1785 is considered by many as a period of decline in religious life. Some speak of it as the "Puritan Decline". We must not, however, think of this period as in direct

---

[1] Stiles, Henry R., The History of Ancient Windsor, Conn., pages 71, 72, 348 Broadway, New York, N. Y., Charles B. Norton, 1859.

contrast to the first period noted for its high idealism, religious fervor and willingness to suffer for a cause. People as a rule do not change their beliefs and habits instantly.

"And, moreover, there are always those so conservatively constituted that they hardly appear to change at all. So that, characterize any given period of history accurately as one may, there are some of its constituent personalities and elements which cannot possibly be brought within its general terms of designation, and which may always be held up as objections to the correctness of that designation."[1]

Still, on the whole this period can only be thought of as a period of decline. There are many reasons for this. The first settlers were united in their purpose of settlement. They expected to form a colony, its laws being based on the teachings of the Bible. In studying about the decline of Puritanism we must consider another group of settlers.

"The descendants, too, of a class of people quite or nearly contemporaneous with the original settlers,—their servants or adventuring hangers-on or followers,—who never had any special sympathy with the high ideals of the real fathers of the New England enterprise, had multiplied as well as the offspring of the founders themselves, and had naturally suffered more even than they from the influences which led to moral decline. They were relatively a numerous, and positively a debassing factor in the life of the colonial towns and villages."[2]

The majority of the early settlers were well educated men and women. The Colonists had made a brave attempt to start schools but with all the other tasks necessary to start new communities education suffered. One has only to read old records to discover the lack of even the knowledge of spelling and simple punctuation among the second and third generation.

This period is also known as the period of land speculation. To get more land was the chief aim of many people. Fiat money was also issued in such large quantities with the result of momentary inflation and collapse of all commercial enterprise.

During this period many of the finest men were killed in the King Philip's War (1675 and 1676) and the Queen Anne's War in 1703.

Nature, not to be outdone, brought many disasters. Believing floods, hurricanes and other catastrophies were caused by the wrath

---

1 Walker, George Lean, Some Aspects of The Religious Life of New England, page 44, New York, N. Y., Silver Burdett and Company, 1897.
2 Ibid, page 49.

of God, in September of the year 1679, the Reforming Synod met at Boston to consider the evils that had provoked the Lord to bring about his judgments on New England.

The churches were beginning to have difficulty. Several churches at this time were divided over the questions of church membership, the location of the meeting-house, or church government. People from the Church of England and various groups of Separatists were asking for more freedom.

The decline in morals may be best shown by extracts from sermons and writings of this period.

"Rev. Samuel Mather of Windsor writing in 1706, says in a pastoral letter addressed to his people:

"It is a time of much Degeneracy . . . In great measure we in this wilderness have lost our first love. . . . We do not walk with God as our Fathers did, and hence we are continually from year to year under his Rebukes one way or other; and yet alas, we turn not unto him that smites us: these considerations call for the utmost of our endeavours, for the reformation of what is amiss amongst us: and for the upholding and strengthening of what yet Remains, and is perhaps ready to dy."[1]

"Across the river, at East Windsor parish in the same town, Rev. Timothy Edwards father of the great Johathan, preached a sermon in May 1712, on a topic upon which the condition of things about them impelled the ministers of Farmington, Hartford, and Windsor unitedly to agree, namely, 'I reverence in the worship of God, and prophanation of his Glorious and fearfull Name by Causless Imprecations and Rash Swearing'."[2]

Rev. Samuel Torrey of Weymouth, Massachusetts preaching the Election Sermon in May, 1683, speaks of the decline of religion in the home.

"How is Religion dying in Families! through the neglect of the Religious Service and Worship of God, and of the Religious Education of Children and Youth and Families. Truly, here, and hereby, Religion first received its death's wound. Hence Religion is dying in all other Societies, among all Orders and Degrees of men, in all ways of Converse, both Civill and Ecclesiastical. O there is little or nothing of the Life of Religion to be seen, or appearing either in the Frame, or Way, Hearts or Lives of the generality of the Professors of it."[1]

---

[1] Walker, George Lean, Some Aspects of the Religious Life in New England, page 72, quoted from Dedicatory Epistle prefaced to the Self-Justiciary Convicted and Condemned, p. 3, 4., New York, N. Y., Silver Burdett and Company, 1897.

[2] Ibid, page 73.

[1] Walker, George Lean, Some Aspects of The Religious Life of New England, page 71, New York, N. Y., Silver Burdett and Company, 1897.

CHAPTER II

THE FIRST CHURCH IN POQUONOCK

The first reference we have of Poquonock is in September 13, 1649.

"This Courte taking into consideracon the many dangers that the families of Thomas Holcombe, Edward Grisswold, all of Wyndsor, are in and exposed unto, by reason of their remoate living from neighbors and neareness to the Indians, in case they should all leave theire families together without any guard; doth free one souldger uppon every training day; each family aforesaid to share herein according to the number of souldgers that are in them: provided that man wch tarryes at home stands about the aforesaid howses uppon his sentinell posture."[1]

The land at Poquonock was soon recognized as excellent soil for farming and settlers soon came. A little settlement grew up in the section now called "Elm Grove".

In 1724 the group at Poquonock petitioned the Assembly for permission to form a separate Ecclesiastical Society.

In May 1724, a committee was appointed by the Assembly to consider the situation at Poquonock and to make report at the next Assembly in October.

In October the General Assembly met at New Haven. Plans for making Poquonock a separate Society were presented. The record reads:

"Upon consideration of the petition of the inhabitants of Pauquannuch in Windsor, praying to be a society of themselves: This Assembly grants they be a society of themselves, and to have such limits and bounds as is described by the committee for that end sent by this Assembly by their act of May last viz; to extend southward as far as Cornelius Brown's including said Brown, and from said Brown's to run a west line to Symbury bounds, and from said Brown's eastwardly a st line to Thomas Thrall's excluding said Thrall, and from said Thrall's or highway to run northwardly to Suffield bounds, abutting east on said road or highway leading to Suffield. And this Assembly do hereby give and grant to the said inhabitants dwelling within the said limits, the powers, and privileges usually granted, to and enjoyed by a society, for the will ordering their affairs, with power to call and settle an orthodox minister among themselves."[1]

---

[1] Hoadley, C. J., and Trumbull, J. Hammond, Colonial Records of Connecticut, Vol. I, page 196, Hartford, Conn., Case, Lockwood and Brainard Company.

[1] Hoadley, C. J., and Trumbull, J. Hammond, Colonial Records of Connecticut, Vol. V, page 489, Hartford, Conn., Case, Lockwood & Brainard Company.

In 1724, the old parish released the forty-four tax payers living in Poquonock.

The new society was incorporated as the third society of Windsor.[2] They invited Mr. Daniel Fuller of Wethersfield to preach here. After hearing him preach a day for ordination was set. Mr. Fuller was never installed as pastor. We do not know the real causes of dissatisfaction between pastor and people. The only light that is shed upon the cause is from one lone record.

"May, 1727. Cornelius Brown testifieth that when Mr. Daniel Fuller was in Poquonnoc, I was one of them that sought for his settlement in ye work of ye ministry there, but perceiving great uneasiness amongst ye people in that affair, and particularly at ye shortness of his sermons, I prayed Mr. Fuller to apply himself to his work, and lengthen out his sermons, that if possible he might gain disaffected persons. Mr. Fuller replied that he did not concern himself about it, if they were but orthodox they were long enough for Poquonnoc.

Cornelius Brown."[1]

Mr. Fuller petitioned the Assembly for redress. He moved his family to Poquonnock and had been put to much inconvenience and expense. Although the Poquonock Society denied having wronged him the Assembly granted Mr. Fuller's request for we read in the Colonial Records:

"Upon the petition of the Rev. Mr. Danll Fuller minister of the gospel the people of the West Society (1) in Windsor, it is resolved and enacted by this Assembly, that said society aforesaid shall pay to the said Mr. Fuller fifty pounds for damages within six weeks after the end of the sessions of this Assembly: and that in failure thereof, the Secretary shall send forth execution for levying the same of them or any of them, and cost, which is allowed to be 4 pounds 9s O. D. Ex. granted August 14th 1727."[2] Later we read:

"Upon the petition of Thomas Griswold, Daniel Griswold and Cornelius Brown, agents for the West Society in Windsor, v Mr. Daniel Fuller: The question being put, whether the pleas offered in bar of said petition are sufficient: Resolved by this Assembly in the Affirmative. Cost Allowed respondent is 20 lbs 18s 6d."[3]

2 There were two churches at Windsor when the Poquonock Society was started.
1 Stiles, Henry R., The History of Ancient Windsor, Conn., page 367, 348 Broadway, New York, N. Y., Charles B. Norton, 1859.
2 Hoadley, C. J., and Trumbull, J. Hammond, Colonial Records of Connecticut, Vol. VII, page 112, Hartford, Conn., Case, Lockwood & Brainard Company.
3 Ibid, Vol. VII, page 141.

In the same year the meeting-house was built. The only records found to date[4] about the early religious life in Poquonock are a few papers from the ministers and a booklet.[1] The booklet reads as though it might be the Ecclesiastical Society Records for it refers only to the financial side of the church.

With the records of the church activities lost we must depend upon the records of the ministers.

Rev. John Woodbridge[2] was the first pastor. He was the fifth Rev. John Woodbridge direct in line from Rev. John Woodbridge a distinguished non-conformist clergyman in England.

"He studied theology and was ordained probably in 1728, as first pastor of the church in Poquonoc, a parish in the north-western part of the town of Windsor, Conn. He laid down his office probably in 1737."[3]

He later moved to south Hadley, Massachusetts. "There he continued until his death, September, 10, 1783 in his 81st year."[4]

"The Rev. B. B. Edwards writing of him fifty-five years after his death says that 'from the recollection of the older inhabitants, his character was that of a prudent and blameless pastor and a sound evangelical preacher'."[1]

While living in Poquonock he lived opposite the present location of Mr. Frank E. Fuller's Gasoline Station.

Unfortunately almost all the records we have with Mr. Woodbridge's signature refer only to money. We have several receipts from him and a paper addressed to the society.

The paper addressed to the society shows that the early minister was not satisfied with the financial support given at Poquonoc.

"To ye Clerk of 3rd Windsor Society to be communicated to Ye Society: Speedily. Whereas my former motions and requests to Ye Society for a comfortable support and maintainance in

---

4 Mr. Allen Mc Leon of Simsbury wrote in a letter (Oct. 16, 1843) that he once had the records of the old Poquonock church.

1 Booklet: See Appendix

2 Rev. John Woodbridge. Geneological information from the Woodbridge Record being An Account of the Descendants of the Rev. John Woodbridge of Newbury, Mass. compiled from the papers left by the late Louis Mitchell Esquire privately printed at New Haven, 1883.

3 Dexter, Franklin Bowditch, Biographical Sketches of the Graduates of Yale College with Annals of the College History, page 344, New York, N. Y., Henry Holt and Co., 1885.

4 Dexter, Franklin Bowditch, Biographical Sketches of the Graduates of Yale College with Annals of the College History, page 344, New York, N. Y., Henry Holt and Co., 1885.

1 Dexter, F. B., Biographical Sketches of the Graduates of Yale College with Annals of the College History, page 345, New York, N. Y., Henry Holt and Co., 1885.

ye work of ye ministry have been disregarded, and have not obtained your due consideration, I thought it best to make a new address to ye Society: not knowing but yt upon my further application, and your own Due Consideration upon Ye Case, you might be moved to something tolerable and yt might be satisfying to me. I would insist upon nothing from you but what is within bounds, both of Reason and Religion. I would not be wanting in applying myself to you before I betake myself to any other means; to you (I say) myself this from him who is a well wisher to your souls, and who has a longing desire to be inhaled by my Lord and Master; and Duly encouraged by your labors to a faithful discharge of ye work of ye ministry among you.

Dated September 11, 1733

Jon Woodbridge."[2]

The society apparently gave Mr. Woodbridge better support for we know that he remained in Poquonock until 1737.

The church was without a pastor for several years. From an old paper we know that the pulpit was supplied by a Mr. Rockwell.

In January 1740, Rev. Samuel Tudor became pastor. He studied at Yale and began his preaching in the Presbyterian Church in Goshen, Orange County, New York. The Synod of Philadelphia appointed October 1735 as the time for his examination. The committee examining him found him insufficient. The text (Romans 11:6) assigned to him may have caused him some difficulty.

The only record of his ministry in Poquonock are a few receipts. He lived north of the Present Elm Grove Mortuary Chapel.

He moved to East (now South) Windsor where he bought a farm. He died there in September 21, 1757 and was buried in the South Windsor Cemetary where his tomb stone may still be seen.

The writing is still legible:

"Here Lies Ye Body of Ye Revd Mr. Samuel Tudor PaFter of one of Ye Churches in WindFsor who departed this Life Septemr Ye 21Ft A.D. 1757 in Ye 52d Year of his Age."

At the time of the pastorate of Mr. Tudor many churches were experiencing revivals. This period is called by some the period of "The Great Awakening". It is not known whether Poquonock had any revivals or not although it is known[1] that Mr. Whitfield preached somewhere in Windsor.

After Mr. Tudor left the Poquonock church was again without a pastor, this time for fourteen years. From receipts found we

---

[2] Manuscript in possession of writer.

know that the Rev. Asabel Hatheway, Ebenezer Gould and Oliver Noble supplied the pulpit.

From the Yale Records[1] we learn that Rev. Ebenezer Gould (or Goold) attended Yale College. He studied theology and in 1728 was ordained and installed pastor of the Presbyterian Church in Greenwich, New Jersey. He was removed from the Presbyterian Church. It is supposed that he died in 1778 or 1779 at East Graville, Hampden County, Massachusetts.

The receipt from Mr. Gould reads as follows:

Windsor, June 9th, 1763.

"Then Recd of the Society Comtee of the Parish of Poquonnoc the Sum of Twenty Two Pounds Ten Shillings lawfull money in full for my Service in the ministry with them from the beginning of the world to this day I say recd by me.

Ebenz Gould."[2]

The fourteen years without a pastor were years of discord. Many did not approve calling a pastor as they did not believe the society could support one. Some desired the society to be dissolved. Petitions to the Assembly to be annexed to Wintonbury[3] or to the old Society[4] were of no avail. Laymen who believed themselves called of God to preach became a disturbing element. There were others who did not care to attend the church in the community. There are records as early as 1754 of Poquonock people supporting the Episcopal Church at Simsbury. Many committees were formed but the society would never agree on any one plan.

On August 1763 a meeting of the society was called for the purpose of inviting Mr. Ambrose Collins to become the pastor. An ordination council was appointed. Just why Mr. Collins never came to Poquonock is not known.

A Mr. Church of Springfield was paid twenty shillings for preaching in 1769.

Finally thirty-six members of the society agreed upon a plan. On January 14, 1771 the following plan was drawn up:

"We, the Subscribers, members of the Second Society of Windsor, Reflecting on the Melancholy state of sd Society in this great Particular, viz.: our having for a long time and still Continuing to be Destitute of a settled minister and some part of ye time without a preached Gospel among us, and also Reflecting on ye

1 Dexter, Franklin Bowditch, Biographical Sketches of the Graduates of Yale College with Annals of the College History, 1st Series, pages 282, 283, New York, N. Y., Henry Holt and Co., 1885.
2 Manuscript in possession of writer.
3 Wintonbury now Bloomfield.
4 Old Society—First Church of Windsor.

great Improbability of ever being able to bring about ye settlement of a Gospel minister in ye Common and ordinary way yt ye Gospel is settled and supported in other Societys, and also being sensible of Ye Solemn obligations yt are upon us to support ye Gospel in a Regular and Honorable way and manner in tenderness to our own souls and those of our Children and friends, and for ye promoting of outward good order among us, have agreed to make one Effort more for the quiet and peaceable Settlement and Support of ye Gospel, hereafter in sd Society, yt is to say for ye Supporting a sound orthodox Dissenting Congregational or Presbyterian Minister.

In consideration of what is above written, we promise to pay our several proportions as Subscribed. Hereunder to a Comtt we shall appoint for ye use above said, when and So long as a Gospel minister remains settled among us and to be by sd Comtt levied and Collected pr annum for ye use above said, by a rate or Tax made on all ye members of sd Society, and Collected in ye usual way and manner as Done heretofore. In witness whereof we have hereunto set our hands this 14th day of January, Anna Domini, 1771."[1]

The following spring Mr. Dan Foster of Stafford was invited to become the pastor of the Poquonnock Church.

Although Rev. Dan. Foster was a pastor of the First Church in Poquonock his belief and teachings represent more nearly those of the next period. His ministry, therefore, will be considered in the next chapter.

---

[1] Manuscript in possession of writer.

CHAPTER III

TRANSITION PERIOD 1775-1818

The period from 1775 to 1818 represents a period of transition. Many changes took place in religion, economics and politics. Puritanism lost much of its dogmatic intolerance and repelling harshness. Congregationalism gradually lost most of its power. Irreligion permeated all ranks of society. The spirit of revolt was wide-spread. There was not only revolt against the rule of the King of England but revolt against all who held back freedom. The various groups of dissenters, religious and political, joined hands until a constitution in 1818 was formed. This constitution was as democratic as any of its time.

Poquonock was very soon influenced by the spirit of revolt. Two men especially are responsible for this. The first one was the minister Rev. Dan Foster who was one of the early Universalist ministers. He not only was liberal in his theoloy but through his writings was an exponent of religious liberty for all. The second person is John M. Niles who did a great deal to create interest in the adoption of the Constitution of 1818.

A. *The Ministry in Poquonock of Rev. Dan Foster*

After many years without a pastor the Poquonock people were happy to have a settled minister.

Plans were made for his ordination which took place in the old meeting-house on June 12, 1771. The ordination was an all day affair judging from the records. People no doubt came from a long distance and, therefore, plans for entertainment were necessary.

A Society meeting was called for on April 23, 1771, "to act upon the following articles of business, viz—

First To Choose a Committee to provide a place for ye entertainment of ye ordaining Council that shall be appointed to ordain Mr. Foster.

21y To Choose Tavernkeepers or submit that matter to ye above said Committee and all business thought proper on said Day respecting Mr. Foster's Ordination."[1]

---

[1] Manuscript in possession of writer.

Two days after the ordination the Society received the following bill.

June 14th Day 1771.

"The Second Society of Windsor, Dr., to Thomas Griswold.

At ordination of ye 12th Day of May Instant—	L	S	d	v
To two gallons of wine at 7s pr gallon	0	14	0	0
To fifty-two meals of victuals at 9d	1	18	3	0
To twelve mugs of flip at 9d pr mug	0	9	0	0
To keeping horses	0	3	0	0
To warning a Society Meeting in 1761	0	0	9	0
	3	5	0	0

Thomas Griswold."[2]

The ordination, however, was not just a time of eating and drinking for the people listened to a very lengthly sermon preached by Rev. Isaac Foster of Stafford, the father of Rev. Dan Foster. The sermon was published and several copies are still in existence.

There were twenty-four members of the church when Rev. Dan Foster became pastor. On the first page of the record book[1] kept by him are the names of eight new members.

During the ministry of Rev. Dan Foster twenty-nine united with the church. Two were excommunicated and at least twelve members died. The largest increase in membership came soon after the adoption of the half-way covenant.

The Poquonock church at a meeting held August 20, 1775 voted:

"That all baptized persons are members of the Christian Church, and subjects of the godly discipline, watch and care of the same; and that it is the incumbent duty of the church to treat them as such."[2]

After this decision fifteen people were admitted to full communion.

The last few years of his ministry were years of friction. There was trouble between the church and the pastor over money[3] and over doctrine.[4]

---

[2] Manuscript in possession of writer.

[1] Record book: Rev. N. G. Bonney in 1881 said that the church book was in existence. It has not been located. The information about the church is from the records copied by Rev. N. G. Bonney and reprinted in the Historical Manual of the Congregational Church, Poquonock, Conn.

[2] Bonney, Rev. N. G., Historical Manual of the Congregational Church, Poquonock, Conn., page 14, Hartford, Conn., Case, Lockwood and Brainard, 1873.

[3] See Appendix   for letters written about financial aid received from church.

[4] See Appendix   for records concerning Rev. Dan Foster and the Hartford North Association.

From an address written by Rev. Dan Foster to an excommunicated person in February 15th, 1778 it seems without doubt that at least when he came to Poquonock he was orthodox in his teachings.

"Nevertheless, we shall not cease to pray for you, that God would have mercy on you, and prevent you in your course of folly and great wickedness, by his Holy Spirit and grace. Take heed, we admonish you, lest being thus bound also in heaven, to your eternal shame and perdition. We leave you in the hands of that God, whose bowels of mercy towards repenting, returning sinners, are infinite, but whose wrath and vengeance towards hardened and persisting sinners are dreadful, and will burn to the lowest hell.

Signed, Dan Foster, Pastor."[1]

Although Rev. Dan Foster came to Poquonock as an Orthodox minister there is no doubt but that he became an exponent of the doctrines of Universalism and freedom of thought for everyone.

His father Rev. Isaac Foster, was deposed, in 1781, from the ministry for preaching Universalist doctrines. At his trial before the Consociation Rev. Dan Foster made a strong plea for more tolerance towards people not of orthodox belief.

Quotations from the paper will help a great deal to understand not only the minister of Poquonock but the viewpoint of the people who were revolting against the authority of the established church.

"Will Americans, true and genuine sons of the fair Goddess Liberty; who have been for several years, and still are, struggling with all the horrors of war, facing the blazing cannon, encountering nameless perils, difficulties, dangers and deaths, to establish here on the throne of these United States, and confirm her falutiserous balmy regency in this land: Will these I ask, subscribe Creeds, Articles of faith, and Confessionals, drawn up and imposed on them by the clergy and ecclesiastick councils and synods! Will they, who neither fled nor submitted at the roar of cannon, and the sound of martial arms in the day of battle, be terrified and awed into submission by the baneless and innoxious thunder of the vatican! Gentlemen, I certainly do not mean to speak diminutively of the clergy, or of ecclesiastical conventions: But I affirm, that no clergyman, or number of clergymen, or ecclesiastick council, of whatever denomination, have right to make religious creeds, canons, or articles of faith, and impose them on any man, or church on earth, requiring subscription to them."[1]

---

[1] Bonney, N. G., Historical Manual of the Congregational Church Poquonock, Conn., page 16, Hartford, Conn., Case, Lockwood and Brainard, 1873.
[1] Foster, Isaac, A Defence of Religious Liberty, page 31, Mass. Bay, Worcester, Printed by Isaiah Thomas, 1780.

His remarks about heretics are very interesting:

"One man is not to be called an heretick, purely because he differs from another, as to the articles of his faith. For then, either we should all be hereticks or there could be no heresy among us. If my neighbor is to be denominated an heretick, purely because he differs from me in his opinions about religious matters, then am I also to be denominated an heretick, because I differ from him in my opinions about religious matters. For certainly I differ from my neighbor in my religious tenets as much as my neighbor differs from me in his."[2]

His father was tried on ten charges of heresy. After his trial Rev. Dan Foster severely criticized the Consocation by saying: "This convention of Consocation is in my humble opinion, wrong, mistaken, unadvited, anti-scriptual, and oppressive."[3]

He then reminds them of the fact that our ancestors fled to this country from ecclesiastical tyranny.

Later on he says:

"This only I say, that however clearly we may think this or the other doctrine to be deduced from scripture, we ought not therefore to impose it upon others, as a necessary article of faith, because we believe it to be agreeable to the rule of faith, unless we would be content also that other doctrines should be imposed upon us in like manner, and that we should be compelled to receive all the different and contradictory opinions of Lutherans, Calvinists, Remonstrants, Anabaptist, and other sects, which the contrivers of symbols, systems, and confessions are accustomed to deliver to their followers as genuine and necessary deductions from the holy scripture."[1]

Two years after Rev. Isaac Foster was deposed from the ministry Rev. Dan Foster was dismissed from Poquonock.

"It seems to be a strange fact that Rev. Dan Foster had a younger brother named Daniel. He, too, and a brother Emerson Foster and a brother John all ministers were dismissed and for the same reason. This being dismissed seems to have run in the Foster family."[2]

It is interesting to note that Rev. Dan Foster's name does not appear on the Poquonock Church roll. He still communed with the Stafford Church.[3]

---

[2] Ibid, pages 40, 41.
[3] Ibid, page 56.
[1] Foster, Isaac, A Defence of Religious Liberty, page 176, Mass. Bay, Worcester, Printed by Isaiah Thomas, 1780.
[2] Letter from Miss Maud G. Booth, Historian of Universalist Church, Stafford, Conn.
[3] He was called to account by the Hartford North Association for this reason.

We learn about the training of Rev. Dan Foster from a letter written by Hosea S. Ballou who writes.

"Rev. Isaac Foster had ten children. Several of his sons studied for the ministry under him, and spread his theology far and wide. The oldest, Rev. Dan Foster, born in 1748, in the spring of 1771 came from Stafford to Poquonock and June 12, 1771 was ordained. His father preached the sermon and it was published. Rev. Dan Foster was a classical scholar. In 1774, both Yale and Dartmouth gave him the honarary degree of Master of Arts. On October 23, 1783, he was dismissed because he preached Universalism, like his father. From 1787 to 1799, Rev. Dan Foster preached and taught at Wethersfield, Vermont, and from 1804 to 1809 at Charlestown, N. H., where he died."[1]

Rev. Dan Foster was before the Association three times. In 1783 and in 1785 he professed to be Calvanistic.[2] He valued and took pains to secure credentials from orthodox minister. Although he tried hard to remove the suspicion placed on him he was unsuccessful, being dismissed from Poquonock October 23, 1783.

Several years after leaving Poquonock he published a book which shows he had changed his theological beliefs from when he entered the ministry. In the Preface he said:

"But, as we are all liable to err, let him reflect that it is as likely he should be mistaken now, in his ideas of the mediatorial dispensation, as that I should have been mistaken in mine, ten or fifteen years ago."[3]

The Poquonock church did not rally sufficiently to call another pastor. The church continued to diminish until 1821 when it became extinct.

B. Growth of Dissent in Poquonock

Movements in thought are always of a much slower growth than the average observer realizes. There are undercurrents of thought which go unnoticed for many years.

To understand the seemingly sudden movement away from orthodoxy we must go back many years. A few dissenters were in the town as early as 1664 when two men (members of the Church of England) requested to be relieved from supporting the established church.

---

1 Dexter, F. B., The Literary Diary of Ezra Stiles. Vol. I, page 248, New York, N. Y., Charles Scribner's Sons, 1901. We read: "And I am told that in June also was ordained at Poquonock Parish in Windsor, Rev. Mr. Foster not of Academic Education." Records of Yale University confirm the fact that Rev. Dan Foster received the Degree.
2 Records from Hartford North Association. See Appendix.
3 Foster, Dan, A Critical and Candid Examination, p iii Walpole, New Hampshire, Thomas & Thomas, 1803.

The dissenters were strong enough so that in 1708 a Toleration Act was passed whereby, they did not have to attend the established church. They were also given the right to have their own churches. They still were compelled however, to support the established church.

1, *Episcopal.* The first record we have of anyone in Poquonock attending church elsewhere is in 1747. The record reads:

"Recd of Shadrack Phelps his rate which was due in the year 1747.

Simsbury May 16th, 1751   William Gibbs
                                                                      Missionary"[1]

From another record signed by William Gibbs we know that seven Poquonock people were attending the Protestant Episcopal Church in Simsbury.

The Society in Poquonock called a meeting on October 3, 1766 "To see what you will Do Relating to those persons Rates that Profess themselves to belong to the Church of England."[1]

2. *The Baptist.* Baptist were among the early dissenters in the town. The section of the town (Pigeon Hill) was the birth place of many very persistent dissenters.

"There was a clerical clan from here a full quartette named Marshall, Daniel and Abraham were father and son, Joseph and Eliakim were twin brothers. Further related[2] I know not. All of them were caught up in the Whitefield whirlwind of the Great Awakening which landed three of them in the Baptist bailiwick and one[3] in jail."[4]

The record concerning Daniel Marshall reads that he became a Baptist and left town. The feeling between the orthodox people and the dissenters is shown also in the funeral service or rather lack of service at the death of Daniel Marshall's wife. The minister refusing to perform the usual service, the people went home leaving the widower to bury his wife.

From Windsor Daniel Marshall went to Georgia. While preaching in Georgia he was arrested by the officers of the Church of England. In spite of opposition he established in 1771 the Kiokee Baptist Church at Appling, Georgia, the first Baptist Church in the State.

---

[1] Manuscript in possession of writer.
[1] Manuscript in possession of writer warning of a Society Meeting.
[2] Daniel Marshall was uncle to Joseph and Eliakim.
[3] Eunice Marshall, a sister of Daniel Marshall, was also put in prison for preaching Baptist Doctrines.
[4] Soule, Rev. Sherrod, Windsor Folks in other Fields, Printed in Booklet Tercentenary First Church Windsor, Conn., page 31.

Of more interest to Poquonock is the work of his son Abraham. On May 10, 1786 he left Georgia for a preaching tour. He kept a diary which was published. He preached in Poquonock several times.

His diary reads: (July 1786)

"Sunday 23. Preached in Poquonock meeting-house at ten o'clock A.M. with considerable ease, to three hundred, at two P.M. to four hundred, and at six P.M. in Broad-street to four hundred and fifty, with great freedom, boldness and courage, as one having authority, and not as the scribes, 'themselves being judges'."[1]

(August 1786)

"Sunday, 6. Preached at Poquonock meeting-house at ten o'clock, A.M. with remarkable freedom to one hundred; and at one, P.M. with greater enlargement, to fifteen hundred. It was supposed that the house had not been thronged so since the Rev. George Whitefield occupied the desk. People attended from five towns, twenty miles distant. Had the third sermon to deliver at five P.M. in Broad-street, in Windsor; hastened down with numbers of his congregation to evening sacrifice; was reenforced by numbers of every rank, so that the whole multitude consisted of about two thousand. It was agreed to do that day what might be termed a miracle: i.e. to open one of the largest meeting-houses in the State, sixty feet by fifty-five, which had been shut and barred against the Dissenters for thirty years. After some consultation, they broke their own law,[2] and opened the 'sanctum sanctorum' for unhallowed feet to tread (i.e. the desk) Here, I thought, Philanthopos forgot himself, and acted the Boanerges in the town of his nativity. Ear-gates gave way, and there appeared a glorious prospect of the Great King Emmanuel's swaying the sceptre over hundreds, and sweetly subjecting them to his easy reign. Who would have thought a lad eleven hundred miles from home, among the most rigid people in the world, would have met with such a reception? But what cannot a God do? Oh that his name may have the praise forever and ever! Amen, and Amen.'

(September 1786)

"Sunday, 10. Preached in Poquonock meeting-house, at ten A.M. on a stage, in a spacious plain; far the largest congregation that ever was seen in those parts on a religious occasion, supposed to be thirty-five hundred. After sermon Eliakim Marshall mounted the stage and gave a clear, striking and powerful account of God's work on his soul, greatly to the satisfaction of the congregation. Also he told them that he had been an advocate for infant sprinkling, in opposition to the primitive order and apostolick mode; that he was now convinced he had no warrant

---

[1] Marshall, Jabez P. Memoirs of the late Rev. Abraham Marshall, page 35. In possession of writer.

[2] Law: No non-resident minister could preach in any parish without the permission of the regular pastor of the parish.

for it in the Bible, and that he was about to comply with the baptism of our Saviour, according to the manner it became him and his followers; which, if they taught and practised with other graces, He would be with them to the end of the world. At two P.M. preached a second sermon; people uncommonly attentive to the word of the Lord; He graced the assembly with his glorious and awful presence; heaven began on earth. Then we advanced through a clover pasture to a river,[1] where Benevolus Philanthropos preached a third sermon on the ordinance of baptism, and then baptized said Eliakim Marshall in the presence of hundreds who had never seen the ordinance administered according to the holy pattern and example of the great Head and Lawgiver, before. After hearing and seeing, some gave their witness that it was right, and were determined to go and do likewise. Others, like the noble Bereans, searched the scriptures to see if these things were so, and some rejected the counsel of God against themselves, not being baptized with the baptism of John. Then returned with E. Marshall, almost worn out, yet rejoicing in the Lord. Preached the fourth sermon in the evening to some friends who came to visit him. Had a happy meeting and evening; said to himself, O Lord, 'I am tired in thy service, but blessed be God, not of it'. Amen.

"11. Attended in Poquonock meeting-house according to appointment, on the ordination of Rev. E. Marshall; the solemnity was profound. It was as follows: Philanthropos made the first prayer, and preached a sermon suitable to the occasion, from Ezekiel i:21: "The spirit of the living creature was in the wheels," to one thousand, who watered the word with a flood of tears; 'some, most of all, because they should see his face no more.' Mr. E. Marshall gave a declaration of his faith in Christ, and call to the work of the ministry. Rev. Hastings made the ordination prayer and gave the charge. Rev. Hamilton gave the right hand of fellowship. Mr. Robins made the concluding prayer. Thanks be to God, it was a good season. Returned to Rev. E. Marshall's and spent the evening very agreeably in company with several friends who came to take one more affectionate farewell of him whom they expected not to see again till the heavens be no more. Remark—One would have supposed that such moments of Abraham's industry and zeal (under the blessing of Heaven) would have elated him to such a pitch of pride that he could not have sustained it. But it is worthy of notice, that such circumstances encouraged him to be still more assiduous and unwearied in well-doing; and to the day of his death, he was an example in being deaf to flatteries and blind to reproaches. May the Lord graciously enable the reader to go and do likewise, so that every one that humbleth himself may be exalted. Amen."[1]

---

[1] River: May have been Stony Brook as the brook was then larger and deeper because of the nearby mill.

[1] Marshall, Jabez P., Memoirs of the late Rev. Abraham Marshall, pages 51, 52. In possession of writer. Printed for the author at Mount Zion, Hancock County, Georgia, 1824.

According to a law of 1784, all people who did not consider themselves Congregationalists were to deposit a certificate of their dissent with the clerk of the Ecclesiastical Society.

There are records which show that Windsor had at least four groups of dissenters: Baptist, Episcopal, Methodist and Universalist.

1. *Baptist*

"This may certify that the subscriber is in Religious Sentiments a Dissenter from the Established Worship of this State to the Baptist Order and she intends Contributing her future share of support to said order.

Windsor, August 9, 1800. Mary Barber."[2]

2. *Episcopal*

"To all persons whom it doth or may concern. This certifies that I Guda Pinney of Windsor in Hartford County heretofore a number of the Second Society of Windsor but differing in sentiments from the worship and ministry in said society and Chuse to join myself to Saint Andrews Episcopal Church in Simsbury and according to law now lodge this my Certificate of which all persons are Requested to take notice.

Guda Pinney.

Dated at Windsor this 12th day of Nov. 179 (?)."[1]

3. *Methodist.*

"I hereby manifest my choice to remain no longer a member of the Second established Ecclesiastical Society in Windsor and have joined myself to the Methodist Society in Windsor. Dated at Windsor this 1st day of January A.D. 1808.

To Abiel Griswold Esqr Clerk of the 2nd Ecclesiastical Society in Sd Windsor.

Gersham Watrous."[2]

4. *Universalist.*

This certificate reads the same as the Methodist one with the exception of course, of the name signed. Although only one Universalist certificate has been found there were several Universalists in the community. Miss Juliet Niles[3] writes that Rev. Dan Foster made several converts among them, Mr. Nathaniel Griswold, Martin Holcomb, and Isaac Griswold.

---

[2] Paper in possession of writer.
[1] Manuscript in possession of writer.
[2] Manuscript in possession of writer. The Methodist and Universalist certificates were printed. The words which were filled in have been underlined.
[3] From record made by Miss Juliet Niles from the recollections of her mother Mrs. Christina Griswold Niles, when nearly ninety-five years of age. Original in the care of the Windsor Trust Co., Windsor, Conn. Estate of Miss Annie Ennis.

C. The Constitution of 1818

The dissenters had many common grieviences. The certificate law was hated by all. Being known as a certificate man placed one at a disadvantage socially and politically.

Education at this time was controlled by the Congregationalists. Until 1798 complete control of the schools was vested in the Congregational Society. The Primary schools opened with prayer and the reading of the Bible. The Congregational Catechism was included in the New England primer. This was taught on Saturday afternoon. In a few instances dissenting children were excused from attending the Saturday session.

The dissenters had many grieviences against the Clergy. They wondered why the Clergy should play such an important part on Election Day. It was noticed that a minister of a denomination such as the Methodist or Baptist seldom preached the Election Day Sermon. Some wondered why so many office holders were related to ministers.

Religious organizations were charged with being politico-religious in their purpose.

"The Bible Society and Ministers' Annuity Society met annually at Hartford on Election Day. As the clergy were there, it proved an excellent opportunity to transact religious as well as civil business. The leaders in these societies were the ruling men of the state. Their lay trustees were Federalist bosses."[1]

There is a group of people we must consider who played an important part in the reform movement. During and after the American Revolution the Deists grew in numbers. Deism was known in America at an even earlier date but it was the war which brought Deistic teaching to the average person.

The French, as America's helpers commanded gratitude and respect.

"Their unorthodox thinking impressed men, and their philosophy was assiduously copied as having a foreign style. Thus the military man on returning from the campaign introduced his newly-acquired habits of thinking and of life among the humble people of his town or wayside hamlet."[1]

The influence of the French Revolution on religious thought was great but it must not be held responsible for all the unbelief. We have seen before the development of a disinterest in religion. The Revolution merely gave a powerful stimulus to deism and reform movements in religion and politics.

Purchell, Richard J, Connecticut in Transition, p. 325, Washington, D. C., American Historical Association, 1918.
Purchell, Richard J, Connecticut in Transition, page 7, Washington, D. C., American Historical Assocation, 1918.

29

Purchell, Richard J, Connecticut in Transition, page 7, Washington, D. C., nerican Historical Assocation, 1918.

The people in Connecticut were also reading letters from their friends in the west where there was more democracy. There was no church tithe and ministers were unimportant there.

The various groups of dissenters united and a Reform Party was started.

One of the leaders of the Reform Party was John M. Niles. He was born in the section of Poquonock called Elm Grove on August 20, 1787. After attending the public schools[2] he studied law in the office of John Sargent. "He wrote many political essays which were published in the "American Mercury" at Hartford."[1] After the war of 1812 he became an ardent worker in the reform movement.

In 1817 he and F. D. Bolles established as a Tolerationist organ, "The Times".[2] For many years he was its editor.

The leaders of the reform movement were considered irreligious. There were two reasons for this. They were not only criticizing religious organizations but had joined hands with deists, Unitarians, infidels etc. The latter three were classed with felons. An article in the "Courant" March 19, 1816, expresses the opinion the advocates of the old order had of the Reformers.

"The leaders of Democracy have for a long time railed at our rulers, our clergy, and our college, but we did not think that they would venture publicly to denounce an institution whose object it is to suppress vice and immorality, or a society whose only object it is, without regard to sect, or nation, to place the pure work of truth and light into every hand within reach."[3]

After many years of struggle a new constitution was adopted. The seventh article dealing with religion was very important. Religion was made voluntary. The day of the certificate man was gone. People no longer were compelled to pay church tithes.

Religion was not destroyed as the Standing Order had predicted. Morally the Congregational Church was helped. People could no longer consider it as tyrannical.

The many groups—the various groups of dissenters, the non-church people and the Republicans felt that now there was freedom for all.

---

2 The present Grammar School is named after him.
1 Howard, Daniel, A New History of Old Windsor, Conn., p. 282, Windsor Locks, Conn., The Journal Press, 1935.
2 The Times now the Hartford Times.
3 Quoted by Purcell, Richard J, Connecticut in Transition, page 325, Washington, D. C., American Historical Association, 1918, from the Courant March 19, 1816.

CHAPTER IV

RELIGIOUS SERVICES HELD IN THE SECOND MEETING-HOUSE

A. *Building of the Second Meeting-House and Early Religious Services Held There*

No building in Poquonock has had as interesting a history as the Second Meeting-House. It was built at a time when the first church in Poquonock was almost extinct. Although there are no regular church books telling about religious services from diaries, letters, newspapers and accounts from older people we find that at least five religious groups held services there.

The building is not standing now but fortunately we have a description of it. The following is the description as given by the late Mr. Albert E. Holcomb.

"It was a large white building. In the front was a large double door. There was a door on the north side also. There were galleries on three sides of the church. Under the galleries were the lights. A stove stood in the center aisle and a pipe went from one side of the stove to the rear of the church. Green wood was burned and pans were hung beneath the pipe to catch the drippings from the wood.

There was a center aisle and on each side of this were square pews. There were also aisles on the right and left sides.

The pulpit was reached by steps afterwards the pulpit was cut down. In the back of the pulpit was a large window and a small one on each side.

Miss Sarah Griswold played the melodian which was in the gallery on the right side towards the pulpit."

Many people wonder how a church can be claimed by several denominations. It is especially confusing when the Second Meeting-House was generally called the Universalist Church although there was no Universalist Society in the Community when it was built. The question arises why was it not called the Congregational Church. There is no question about the first church being Congregational* but we must remember that the church did not build the Meeting-house.[1] The meeting-house was the place of worship but that was only one use made of it. There was little if any "hallowed

---

* Remembering of course the close connection between the Congregationalist and Presbyterians. A few people called it a Presbyterian Church.

[1] In all fairness to Rev. N. G. Bonney who claimed the Society which built the Meeting-House was Congregational it should be stated that the majority who paid for the building were Congregationalists at the time. Many of the family's names, however, appear later among the Universalists.

attachment" to the meeting-house. It was built and supported by the Ecclesiastical Society (one did not have to be a church member to belong). The meeting-house was literally the "meeting-house", all public meetings being held there. It served as church building, town hall and recreation hall.

The Second Meeting-House was apparently started in 1797 for then a Committee was appointed to make use of any of the old building for the new.

The Meeting-House was finished by a tax and subscription for in a record of the Second Society we read:

"We the subscribers, inhabitants of the Second Society of Windsor taking into consideration the vote that has this day been passed to raise a tax towards finishing the Meeting-House in said society and feeling ourselves willing to contribute something more than our tax towards finishing said House do hereby bind ourselves to pay to Capt Isaac Pinney, Treasurer for said society the severall sums annexed to each of our names to be applied for the purpose of finishing said meeting-house (in case two hundred and fifty Dollars is subscribed) which sums or articles we severally bind ourselves to pay by the 15th day of October next on condition that said 2nd Society of Windsor do not reconsider or disanule the vote this day passed for raising a tax; but if said society do refuse to collect said tax and apply the same is voted by the first day of October next then the above instrument to be null and void otherwise to remain in full force and virtue in the Law. Dated at Windsor, Dec. 3rd, 1799."[1]

The following page gave the list of the subscribers and the amount pledged. Two hundred and sixty-six (or sixty) dollars was pledged and all but fifteen dollars (three pledges) were marked paid.

The first religious services held in the Second Meeting-House were conducted by ministers from the Association. We read in the Minutes of the Hartford North Association February 3, 1801 that ministers were appointed to preach in Poquonock during April, May, and June.

Rev. David Austin preached there about a year (1806?). The Rowland family were very much concerned about the religious life of the community. Meetings were held from 1816 to about 1822 with the Rowlands or the Soper family. Many of the people who preached were from the Center Church, Hartford.

Poquonock was beginning to lose its fine reputation. Some referred to it as Sodom and Gomorrah.

---

1 Manuscript in possession of writer. First page missing.

A letter written in 1827 helps us to realize that although there was no church organization there were church services. The first reference to Sunday Schools is in this letter. The writer of the letter in defending Poquonock writes as follows:

"You alluded something in your first letter you wrote me since your residence in New York concerning the corrupt, wicked society of Poquonock. You are under a great mistake. This Parish, it is true, has borne that name but it has greatly improved since your departure. We have Preaching regular every Sabbath in which the Congregations are as large as can be expected from so small a parish. The denominations which we have preaced to us are a Presbyterian and a Methodist. The Presbyterian preaches one half and the other the Methodist. Furthermore we have a Sabbath School established in which between thirty and forty Children attend. This is considered the greatest improvement that has yet been made in this Sociey. I not only serves to keep the Children from rambling the fields on the Sabbath stealing fruit from their neighours but also stores their minds with useful knowledge, which in point of time may bring them in the right road that will make them happy after this life."[1]

About the same time a committee was appointed in the Ecclesiastical Society for the purpose of procuring evangelical preaching.

One of the leaders was Mr. Samuel Hollister who had started business with Mr. Niles. Mr. Hollister, had noticed the newly painted building and taken it for granted that services were maintained.

Methodist and Baptist preachers were first employed. From Mr. Marshall's letter we know that Presbyterian ministers also preached.

A vote was taken in the Society and the people were in favor of Congregational preaching by a majority of one. Rev. Mr. Brinsmade of Hartford supplied the pulpit for several months.

The Congregationalists held their services in Poquonock and Rainbow.

The majority of the people in the section of the town near the meeting-house were Universalists. They were not newcomers but descenants of the people who were influenced by the preaching of Rev. Dan Foster.

---

[1] Letter (Sept. 30, 1827) from David Marshall (age 18) to Francis S. Latham. In possession of writer.

B. The Universalist Society of Poquonock

1. *Early Universalists in Connecticut.* The Universalist was the most disliked and misunderstood by the Congregationalist of the several groups of reformers and dissenters. The Methodists, Episcopalians and Baptists were at least orthodox in theology. There were two main criticisms of the Universalists. They were Democrats[1] (with a few exceptions) and by preaching Universal Salvation discounted one of the essential doctrines of Calvanism. The orthodox felt that an oath should not be accepted from them anymore than from a Deist or Infidel because it lacked the restraining fear of a future life.

As early as the year 1802 Universalism and Unitarianism had gained sufficient power for the orthodox churches to become alarmed. The Hartford North Association emphasized the importance of indoctrinating the young people.

A few years later the question whether or not Universalists should be allowed to receive communion was discussed.

2. *Universalist ladies organizations in Poquonock.* The Universalist Society of Poquonock was one of the earliest[1] in the state.

The oldest records are of a Ladies Charitable Society. In 1833 a group of ladies met together to organize "The Universalist Ladies Sewing Society". At one of their first meetings they decided that they should spend their time in worthwhile activities for the community. The name was then changed to the "Poquonock Ladies Charitable Society". It was still to be a sewing society but the articles made were to be given to needy people in the community.

It would be interesting to know how well they lived up to their first by-law which read:

"Conversation should be at all times, as it becometh the Gospel of Christ, hence the members, at all meetings of the Society, do agree to refrain entirely from remarks which are calculated to injure the Character of any person whether present or absent, being resolved that when no good thing can be said of others the tongue shall be silent in reference to them."[2]

A large basket[1] was placed in the church. The clothes made by the ladies were placed in it and given away when the need came.

---

1 Democrats refers to Democratic-Republican Party (The Reform Party)

1 Earliest newspaper clipping (Poquonock News) entitled "New Mortuary Chapel", Hartford, Connecticut, The Post, January 15, 1894. The article refers to the Society having existed over one hundred years.

2 Manuscript "Constitution and Records of the Poquonock Ladies Charitable Society", loaned by Mrs. Elsie Alford Bensenhaver.

1 Basket owned by Mrs. Alice Holcomb Phelps.

34

The Society also sewed for people in the community who were able to pay for the work being done.

The men in the community were soon interested in the organization and supported it financially.

The attendance of ladies not members of the Society is mentioned several times. Women from Windsor became interested in the work and attended several meetings helping with the sewing.

The last record[2] is of a meeting held on March 12th, 1835.

In 1848 the Universalist Ladies Sewing Society[3] was organized. The constitution reads (with almost no change) the same as the constitution of the Poquonock Ladies Charitable Society.

The name Sewing Society is misleading in many ways. From its records we know that it was a general church organization. It had thirty-nine active members and forty-four honorary members. Many of the honorary members were men.

The main purpose of the organization seems to be the raising of funds to support the society. The women met every two weeks and sewed. The money received from the garments (orders were taken) was used for church purposes. Several methods of raising money were used besides the first one.

The people were more dependent upon the local communities for their social activities than now. The Universalist Society rented Elm Grove Hall[1] several times for socials. One festival alone brought in $144.22. Money was raised also by lottery and fortune telling. Another method used was fining the members for non-attendance at meetings. Judging from letters, records and diaries written during this period it was a time of many social activities.

3. *Religious services.* Although no church records have been found we know that for many years there was preaching in the Second Meeting-House by Universalist ministers.

From letters,[2] the Account Book and Minutes of the Universalist Ladies Sewing Society we find the following accounts of money spent for religious purposes.

1845, July, Books for the Sunday School	$10.00
1848, July, Books for the Sunday School	10.00
1848, July, For support of the Gospel Ministry	20.00
1849, Cash paid for preaching	20.00

[2] They may have had other meetings. There is no record of the organization disbanding.

[3]. The Universalist Ladies Sewing Society may be the Ladies Charitable Society reorganized.

[1] Elm Grove Hall now Elm Grove School.

[2] Letters written to Mr. Eli Phelps from the following ministers: Rev. C. R. Moore, Rev. A. Norwood, and Rev. L. A. Davis.

1850, July 11, Cash, Rev. W. L. Ballou for pre preaching	5.00
Sept 1, Mr. Moore for preaching	8.00
_____ Rev. J. H. Farnsworth	20.00
1851, Sept. 15, Mr. Eli Phelps[3] for preaching	5.00
1852, Pulpit supplied by Rev. A. Norwood.	
1854, August 20, Mrs. Williams for Melodians	$70.00
October 10, Paid Timothy Phelps for singing	15.00
1856, May for preaching	12.00
1857, Feb. 25, Paid for dyeing fringe for pulpit	.50
1857, April 23rd, Paid Mr. Haskins for preaching	55.00
1858, Jan., Paid Mr. Allen	15.00
March 7, Paid Mr. Allen	10.00
July 28th, Paid for Bible for church	5.50
August, Mr. Moore	13.00
Mr. Hickning	15.00
Sept. 1, Sabboth School Books	12.00
Sept. 14, Mr. Allen for preaching	52.00
1862, Paid Mr. Allen	50.00
1866, Paid Mr. Allen	50.00
1867, Paid Mr. Davis	10.00
1873, Dec. 18th, Voted to pay Mr. Davis	10.00

4. *The Elm Grove Mortuary Chapel*. Although the meeting-house was torn down[1] in 1872 the Universalists continued to have services in private homes and at Elm Grove Hall. They raised money by having balls, lectures, and entertainments. This money with that received from offerings was deposited in a bank. The money finally amounted to fifteen hundred dollars. Some of the ladies suggested that the money be used to build a Mortuary Chapel.

The foundation was built by the Second School Society.[2] The building cost $2000. Miss Juliet Niles gave the needed $500. When the building was given to the Second School Society provision was made for the Universalists using the building for services.

On the wall to the north of the pulpit is a brass tablet, cruciform in shape, bearing the following inscription: "The ladies of the Universalist Society built this Chapel and gave it to the Second Society."

[3] Mr. Eli Phelps records are sometimes misleading. He paid the ministers from society money.
[1] Only a few inhabitants opposed it being torn down. It was in need of a great deal of repair. The building was not sold but given to the person who tore it down. It was rebuilt and used for many years as a farm building on the Marshall Farm.
[2] Second School Society has charge of Elm Grove Cemetery.

The building was dedicated January 15, 1894 with the following service:

"Organ   Voluntary   Mrs. T. B. Hathaway.
Reading   Nineteenth Psalm   Rev. N. T. Merwin.
Prayer   by Rev. Mr. Davis of Hartford.
Solo   "Sweetly, Solemn Thought", by Mrs. George
                              F. Wilbraham.
Address, by Rev. N. T. Merwin, in which he descanted on the future use of the new building, and contrasted the ancient and modern methods of disposing of the dead.
Solo   "Flee as a bird" by C. Robert Hatheway.
Address by Rev. Mr. Davis of Hartford, which was replete with anecdotes and in which the Universal brotherhood of man was forcibly commended.
Solo, "Send out thy light", by Miss Florence Clark.
Possession of the building given by Mr. Henry A. Huntington (on behaft of the Ladies Society) to Hon. George W. Hodge representing the Second School Society.
Doxology
Benediction   Rev. Mr. Davis."[1]

5. *Disbanding of the Universalist Society.*   The Universalist Society may have never officially disbanded.   The last record of the Society is that in 1915 the three surviving members turned over to the Second School Society $141.98.   The last member of the society Mrs. Ida G. Strickland died in 1935.

Some of the Universalists joined the new Congregational Church started at Poquonock Center in 1841.   The majority of them, however, joined the Spiritualist Society.

C. *The Spiritual Harmonical Society of Poquonock*

The Spiritual Harmonical Society of Poquonock is one of the oldest in the country.   One of their leaders, Mrs. Flavia Thrall attracted much attention.   She was born in Windsor on May 28, 1838, daughter of Mr. and Mrs. Cyrus Howe.

"As a child she manifested powers beyond the ordinary, but so far were they then misunderstood that her parents regarded them with uneasiness, fearing them as evidence of mental blight. Her clairvoyant power was characterized by herself in childish phrase as 'seeing away off'.   At the age of fourteen her ability as a healer was revealed to her, and, having accepted the call to this high service, she has practiced for forty-seven years, during which she has performed some of the most remarkable cures on record."[1]

---

[1] Newspaper clipping, Poquonock news, entitled "New Mortuary Chapel" from The Post, Hartford, Conn., January 15, 1894.
[1] Commemorative Biographical Record of Hartford County, Conn., p. 961, Chicago, Illinois, J. H. Beers & Co., 1901.

Mrs. Thrall soon gained a reputation as a healer not only in Windsor but in every state and in Europe. She was consulted by people of other beliefs. Among the people who consulted her were clergymen, lawyers and doctors. Mrs. Thrall and Mrs. Isadora Strickland (another Poquonock medium) had regular doctor's licenses.

The Spiritualist organization first met in homes, then in the Meeting-House at Elm Grove. Later they built Liberal Hall in Poquonock. Their history has been well told by Mrs. Flavia Thrall.

"History of the Early Days of Spiritualism, The Society at Poquonock—a Half Century of Reminiscenses.

"Fifty years ago a little gathering of friends was at the home of Cyrus Howe one evening, ostensibly for a social call and general pleasant time. During the evening a Mr. Billings of Somerville, Connecticut, called at the house to stay overnight. He was introduced to the callers and thereupon asked Mr. Howe if the assembled folks might have a 'sitting'.

" 'Sitting,' said Mr. Howe in amazement, 'why of course we'll have a sitting, you don't expect to stand do you?'

"Hereupon the gentleman who made the suggestion explained that he referred to the sitting of the folks present in a circle about a table for spiritual manifestation. The gentleman seated himself at a table and called different ones to come and put their hands upon the table. There was no appreciable success of spiritual manifestations until your humble servant,[1] then a little girl, was requested to place her hands upon the table, when to the astonishment of those present, the table rose immediately and was suspended in the air, returning to the floor whence it performed through my agency many peculiar antics familiar to people of later day Spiritualism. These were the initial manifestations of spiritual phenomena in Poquonock, Conn. This occurred about three years after the Rochester rappings[2] that had made such a sensation.

"From this start many became interested, circles being held at our home and elsewhere with enthusiastic regularity. Some of the early members were Mrs. Salmon Clark, whose spiritual nature seemed so fully developed as to accept all the liberal ideas developed by spiritual philosophy, her confidence and trust in spiritual knowledge and goodness of soul are remembered by all who knew her. It was at her home the knowledge of my gift as a clairvoyant first came to me. Her baby was seriously ill at the time, I became entranced and prescribed for the child, to whom she gave the medicine, and her recovery was remarkable. That first patient, now Mrs. Eliza Lamberton, is and has been, Secretary of our Society for a number of years.

---

[1] Mrs. Flavia Thrall.
[2] See Lyman, Dwight A., Rappings of Peddler's Ghost Became the Foundation of Modern Spiritism, The Hartford Daily Times, August 6, 1921, page 5.

"Some of the early investigators were the Thrall family, Mrs. Warren Griswold, Mrs. A. P. Williams, Shelby Clark and family, Mrs. F. M. Brown of Windsor Locks, David Pinney and family, Dr. Chaffee, Joseph Whipple and family. One of his daughters, Mrs. Strickland is still a member of our society. We continued our circles and investigations, the interest and attendance increasing until we decided to call lecturers to receive all the best advantages possible of the philosophy of Spiritualism. The first lecturer called was Warren Chase. Mr. Chase was a Congressman, and a lecturer of great ability. Following was Dr. John Mahew, Frank Wadsworth, N. Frank White, Mrs. Fannie Burbank Felton, Prof. S. B. Britton, all able exponents of harmonical philosophy of those days.

"After ten years of patient work in this good cause, it was proposed by Cyrus Howe, my father, nearly 80 years of age, to form an organization to assist us spiritually and financially, for in unity there is strength. This proposal being favorably received Dec. 5, 1861, he formulated the constitution and by-laws of the Spiritual Harmonical Society, of which, today, we are celebrating the fortieth Anniversary.

"There were originally about sixty members, the majority of which have passed over to the other life, and often cheer us by the communications which we receive in our circles.

"In those days the occurrence of the Rochester Rappings had left a deep impression on us, because of their import. It became our custom to celebrate the anniversary of the phenomena regularly each year, March 31st being the day, from far and near assembled the friends of our Cause at some appointed home of a Spiritualist. No matter how inclement the weather, mud bespotted seekers of the truth laboriously toiled through mud and slush to be on hand, as it were.

"In the early days among the other lecturers we had Miss Nettie Coburn, who became Mrs. Nettie Coburn Maynard, and who was attached to Pres. Lincoln and wife in capacity of medium. She worked and developed with us two years prior to going to Washington. Mrs. Maynard was the author of the work 'Was Abraham Lincoln a Spiritualist?' Mrs. Maynard was one of our most remarkable mediums.

"About this time occurred the development of John O. Phelps, who possessed remarkable healing powers, and did so much good for all about him. Mr. Phelps' personality was a ready recommendation of the truth of his mediumship to all who knew him. Many new ones became interested at this time. Mr. Nelson Bowers, being controlled to give many beautiful thoughts from the other world, bringing more members. Mr. Joseph Hungerford, the Clark families, Mr. Chauncey Newberry, and many others being brought to the truth. Mr. Hungerford was a more than willing worker with great executive ability.

"After nearly twenty years of true and earnest work the building of a hall seemed a necessity, as we had no place to hold our lectures, except the old Universalist church. To heat this comfortably for us[1] one cold December night the young men across the river, a mile and a half away, brought wood in their arms to burn in the old box stove that stood in the centre aisle, around which we clustered and kept our faces warm, while we listened to the words of inspiration from our speakers. I mention this fact to show the enthusiasm of our work in those days. We held our socials at the homes of different members. We continued our lectures, employing the best speakers obtainable, including Laura De Force Gordon, Amanda Spence, Anna Hinman, Cephas B. Lynn, Lizzie Doten, L. B. Miller, Professor Eccles, J. Frank Baxter and many others.

"By holding socials and fairs and with gifts of money and work from those interested, we were able to build a hall.

"In 1879 the hall was erected, which we now occupy. Mrs. Brigham was present at the dedication. We now hold regular fortnightly socials for exchange of thought and progressive ideas and a general harmonical gathering.

"In the early days we had much opposition to encounter because of our strange belief, but we paid but little heed to it. I well remember people would talk with my father and endeavor to persuade him of his folly. But his advanced ideas concerning a future existence caused them to see the futility of their attacks, and they soon ceased. One of the most bitter assailants of free thought in this vicinity was deacon Roger Phelps, of Windsor. On one occasion he called upon Mr. Howe and a long debate followed upon capital punishment. When leaving the house Deacon Phelps exclaimed:

" 'O! how I long for the good old days of Salem witchcraft, I would have Howe's girl hung to the nearest apple tree.'

"In return Mr. Howe characterized him as 'another of the many fossils he had to encounter'."

The Spiritual Harmonical Society still exists and occasionally holds meetings. It is incorporated with a board of directors. The group although a religious group is not organized as a church. Many of its members are members of the Poquonock Congregational (Community) Church.

---

[1] Across the river—the Thrall family lived there.

CHAPTER V

SOCIAL AND EDUCATIONAL ORGANIZATIONS NOT DIRECTLY CONNECTED WITH THE CHURCH

After the Constitution of 1818 many of the people thought that religion was doomed. It is true that the rigid Calvanism of the early churches was passing. Although in many communities the Congregational Church gained power, in many places another group were in the majority. These people were nominally Congregationalist. Some of them joined other religious groups but the majority of them became what Rev. Ezra Stiles called "Stay-at-home Protestants".

These people still accepted the teachings of Christianity but were much more concerned with present social and economic problems than with doctrinal and more definitely religious matters. An interest in libraries, governmental problems, social questions and education in general was developed.

A. *The Poquonock Philosophical Debating Society*

On March 13, 1822 a group of young men met in the schoolhouse to form the Poquonock Philosophical Debating Society. The purpose of the organization was to

"store their minds with useful knowledge. They agreed to meet together and discuss problems of a Philosophical and Literary nature. In Article nine they agreed that, 'Religious controversies shall be avoided also such political questions as would ... create party spirit'."[1]

Rules of conduct were also made. No member was allowed to drink or use profane and obscene language.

Although membership in the organization was limited to men, the records indicate that women attended at least some of the meetings. The discussions were apparently very animated and prolonged. A rule was finally made whereby no person could speak more than one hour at a time.

The topics discussed at their meetings were:

1. Whether Hartford County Agricultural Society is of any benefit to the County.

2. Whether or not a man owning a Grain Store ought to turn ... Brandy and cider or not.

---

[1]

"The Judgement that owners of Grain stores ought to turn . . .
Brandy and Cider and may God have mercy upon their poor
souls."

3. Which affords the greatest pleasure Anticipation or Parti-
cipation.

4. Is there such a thing as Patriotism?

5. Whether or not Lamphrey Eels are of any benefit to Poquonock.

6. Which is the most utility to the United States Commerce or
Manufacturies.

7. Which has caused most bloodshed, Religion or Politics.

B. Young Men's Debating Society of Poquonock

The manuscript found gives very little information. There is
no date or even one name on the paper. The value of the meager
record is that it shows the beginning of interest in a library and
in Temperance.

The three topics discussed were:

"1· Is it expedient to establish a social library in this place on
any convenient and popular plan?

"2. Ought spirituous liquors to be considered and used only as
a dangerous medicine?

"3· Is it expedient that there should be any united exertions
made in this place for the promotion of temperance?"[1]

C. Libraries in Poquonock

1. *Poquonock Social Library.*[2]   The library was organized on
January 14, 1828. It was a stock company, each share costing five
dollars.

The rules made were as follows:

"Fines shall be imposed by the Committee or Librarian agreeable
to the following estimates.

Soiling, one cent to three a page.

Oil spots, two cents to six for each leaf.

Tearing and other damages and losing at the discretion of the
Committee or Librarian according to the damage sustained by
the society."

In 1849 the organization was dissolved and the books were divided among the stock owners. There were two hundred and eighty-
eight books. They were on history, philosophy, government, a few
on nature and one on religion, "Ultra Universalism".

---

[1] Manuscript, Young Men's Debating Society of Poquonock, in possession of
the writer.

[2] Poquonock Social Library records in possession of the writer.

2. *Poquonock Union Library*. The only record of the library is a paper giving the by-laws. One of the by-laws was that it should be near the Center. This may be the library which was located in Buck's Hall[1] about 1870. Each member paid one dollar or one dollar and a quarter each year and was allowed to borrow one book a week.

3. *Public Library*. The first free libraries in the town were the Sabbath School Libraries. Although they were free they cannot be considered as public libraries as they were established for the Sabbath School pupils. The first public library was started in 1888. Poquonock has a branch library named in memory of its first librarian, Mrs. Emma K. Hatheway.

D. *Temperance*

Poquonock during the early part of the nineteenth century had a reputation for being a place where Sabbath breaking and intemperance were common.

The church people tried to remedy the first fault by having church services not only at Elm Grove but at Poquonock Center and Rainbow.

The first temperance work was about 1830 when a Mr. Hunt spoke. The first evening the audience was very noisy but the speaker finally won the attention of the group. He spoke two other evenings. About eighty people joined and signed the temperance pledge.

Poquonock Center had a "revival" in 1841. About this time there was also a great interest in Temperance. It is estimated that two hundred signed the pledge. The social life of the community was soon affected. In former years cider brandy[1] was served at the parties, but temperance balls were now given. At least one young person did not approve of light drinks for refreshments. In a letter to a friend she writes:

> "There is to be a ball here Friday night, a temperance ball. Isn't it facitious but I shall not go, as it would be too bad not to have the pleasure of even a sip just the bubbles of champagne and I will not countenance anything so ridiculous. Besides I should die with the stupidity. I reckon there will only be married people present who can get along very well with cold water, and are not expected to be agreeable."[2]

Buck's Hall was built for a railroad station by Mr. Daniel Buck when it was oped the railroad would come to Poquonock. The room upstairs contained ballroom. The building stood almost opposite where the First National tore in Poquonock is located.

Cider brandy—there was a distillery near Elm Grove Hall.

Letter (1845) in possesion of writer. Name of writer of letter withheld.

There are people still living who can remember temperance meetings in Buck's Hall. Speakers came from Hartford. The group was spoken of as the "Blue Ribbons". When the pledge was taken a Catholic Priest came and had a service. It is not known just how many signed the pledge. Interest was so high that, according to reports, only one man failed to sign the pledge.

There were several names given to the Temperance Societies. In 1873 Poquonock had a Good Templars Lodge. A letter written to a Poquonock girl refers to the Lodge as being in a prosperous condition.

Later we read of the Windsor Temperance Union. They were very much concerned about having Windsor vote "No license". One of their circulars read:

"Windsor, Conn., Oct. 1, 1885.

Dear Sir:

Perchance you have a father, brother, son. relative or friend whom you would save from intemperance and the dangers of the Rum Shop. We implore you, therefore, to support the cause of law and order. Vote No license on Monday next, and influence your fellow citizens to act likewise.

Yours Fraternally,

The Windsor Temperance Union."[1]

Another Temperance Organization was called the "Good Samaritan". It was organized on March 31, 1887. Mr. Pettibone, the Congregational minister, and Mr. Temple, the Baptist minister, took an active part. The group apparently had a . . . service for they had a choir and singing books, but the meetings were also social gatherings.

The Catholic men had a Temperance Society called the Total Abscience Benevolence Society.[1] Meetings were held in Franklin Hall from June 3, 1894 to December 1895. The meetings generally ended in discussions and debates.

---

[1] Manscript in possession of writer.
[1] Total Abscience Benevolence Society Record Book in possession of Mr. Thomas J. Connor, Main Street, Poquonock Conn.

THE BAPTIST CHURCH

A. The Baptist of Rainbow

About 1858 a small group of people started Baptist services in the village of Rainbow. Their early history is best told by the oldest living member of the former Baptist Church.

"Prayer meetings were started in Rainbow about the year 1858 by George L. Hannah, Mr. Hodge and my father and mother and at the request of Mrs. Harlow Moore, a member of the Congregational Church at Poquonock, and held at her house. These meetings were continued till the death of G. L. Hodge in 1869. While on his deathbed said Hodge called his two sons G. W. Hodge and William C. Hodge together with his son-in-law J. J. Merwin, also a nephew W. L. Bidwell and got their promise that a Baptist Church be built at once at Rainbow. G. L. Hodge passed on March 23, 1869. 1st meetings were begun in the Hall[1] owned by my father. The first sermon was preached by Emry Shailer of Deep River, Conn., who was serving the State as Baptist Missionary at the time and a dear friend of my father."[2]

The group was organized into a church May 18, 1875 and officially recognized by the Baptist Convention.[3]

Meetings were held in the hall until 1879 when a church building was started. The church stood south of where Mr. Michael Hayden lives. His home is the former Baptist parsonage. The church was dedicated about 1881.

The church prospered for a time. People attended from East Granby and Poquonock as well as Rainbow. There were two services on Sunday besides the Sunday School. Every Christmas there was a party and a tree with presents for the children. A Mission Band was organized. This group of children read missionary stories and also contributed to missions. A Chatauqua Literary and Scientific Society was organized. People from other churches were also members of this study group.

Many of the Baptists were very strict, even disapproving of eating food on Sunday. When church suppers were started one lady said that money changers were being brought into the Lord's

---

[1] This was no doubt the building called the Chapel. There are several people living who remember Baptist services being held there.

[2] Letter from W. C. Hodge of Deep River, Conn. 1935

[3] Connecticut Baptist Convention Minutes of the 52 Annual Meeting of the Connecticut Baptist Convention, Hartford, Conn., Case, Lockwood and Brainard, 1875.

45

House. Wishing to contribute to the church, she would bring her money to the road near the church, and one of the ladies from the church would come and receive her contribution.

The story is told that at the close of one of the meetings, how some business matters were to be considered, someone noticed that there were two people not members of a Baptist Church; whereupon one lady said, "I move that the world be dismissed."

The exact date of the discontinuing of Baptist services is not known. In a report of the Congregational Church 1894 we read:

"The introduction of Catholic help in the factories has weakened the Congregational Church and practically broken down the Baptist Church of Rainbow, where a pretty edifice was built a few years ago by aid of Elder Jennings of Deep River. Worship has been [given] up. Only seven members remain in the place of whom several attend the Congregational Church. They do not expect to resume worship. A fine omnibus runs on Sunday from Rainbow to the Congregational Church A.M. and P.M."[1]

The Baptist Church was bought by the Wilson Christian Union Association in 1900. It was rebuilt at Wilson the same as it was in Rainbow.

From letters, newspaper articles and minutes of organizations we know that the following were pastors at Rainbow.

Rev. A. S. Burrows. The church was started during his ministry.

Re. William Hansell, D.D. The church was officially recognized during his ministry, therefore, he was in Rainbow as early as 1875.

Rev. Daniel F. Chapman.

Rev. Mr. Temple. He was at Rainbow in 1887 as we find him referred to in the minutes for 1887 of the Good Samaritan Society.

Rev. George W. Hinckley.

Rev. T. G. Wright. He was the last pastor.

The money of the rainbow Baptist Church was given to the Judson Memorial Church in New York City.

There had always been a friendly spirit between the Baptists and the Congregationalists of the community. After the Baptist Church disbanded the group attended the Congregational Church.

---

[1] Report from Congregational Church June 25, 1894. Report now at the Congregational House, 37 Garden Street, Hartford, Connecticut.

CHAPTER VII

THE CATHOLIC CHURCH

A. *St. Joseph's Catholic Church*

The first Catholics in Poquonock were Irish people who came here to work in the mills. Although they were few in number they were soon able to have Catholic services.

For the early records of Catholic services in Poquonock we are dependent upon the records of St. Mary's Parish in New Britain. It had jurisdiction over Plainville, Bristol, Farmington, Avon, Tariffville and Rainbow. From 1848 to 1852 Catholic services were held in Rainbow in the building called the Chapel. Before Catholic services were started one man used to walk from Rainbow to Hartford, a distance of eleven miles, to attend mass.

"In 1852 Rainbow and Poquonock were placed under the jurisdiction of St. Mary's Parish in Windsor Locks. In "The Catholic Church in Connecticut" by Monsignor Duggan, the fact is mentioned that in 1848 Father Brady of Hartford, Poquonock used to minister to the Catholics there."[1]

In 1852 Father Smyth secured the Holy Name Hall for a meeting place. Services were also held in Franklin Hall. A few Catholic services were held in the home of Mr. Nugent on Maple Avenue until a hall was secured.

The present church was built in 1887. At the laying of the cornerstone a collection was taken. It was estimated to be over one thousand dollars. Community interest in the church was shown by the fact that Protestants as well as Catholics contributed towards the building fund.

In 1892 Poquonock became a separate parish. The church at Windsor Center became a parish of the Poquonock Church. It became a separate parish in 1921, then became a mission of the Poquonock Church instead of St. Mary's Church of Windsor Locks. In 1921 it became a separate parish.

It is interesting to note that about the same time the Poquonock church became a separate parish another group of people settled in the community. In 1891 the first Lithuranians came to Poquonock. Soon many came to work in tobacco. They were Catholics and helped the Catholic Church to develop. Provision is made for the group who are helped by having services conducted in their

---

Letter to writer from Rev. John Connor, St. Mary's Hospital, Waterbury, Conn., March 16, 1936.

own language. The group also has a Benefit Society organized in 1910. This organization is not conducted with the church.

Since St. Joseph's became a separate parish it has been served by the following pastors:

The Rev. John Fleming, 1892 to 1898.

The Rev. Thomas Shanley, 1898 to 1900.

The Rev. Francis L. Lally, 1900 to 1911.

The Rev. John J. Fitzgerald, 1911 to 1916.

The Rev. John F. Quinn, 1916 to 1921.

The Rev. Edward J. Plunkett, 1921 to 1930.

The Rev. Patrick L. Dolan, 1930.

The Rev. Joseph A. Healey, owing to the absence of Father Dolan, has had the care of the parish, which now includes more than seven hundred. He supervises the religious education program. There are three classes in religious education for children. The High School boys and girls meet in the afternoon. They write articles about what they are studying and must be able to defend what they have written. Some of the boys are trained to be Altar Boys. The girls are organized into "The Children of Mary". The women have a Ladies Altar Society which takes care of the Altar and Sanctuary.

The Social life of the Young People is also considered. The boys and girls have basketball teams called St. Casimirs. There is also a St. Joseph's Dramatic Club. The town hall is used for the basketball games and the plays.

The church is fortunate in that it not only has a church building but has the Holy Name Hall near by which is used for weekday activities.

CHAPTER VIII

THE POQUONOCK CONGREGATIONAL CHURCH

A. *Early History of Congregational Preaching 1835-1854*

The organization of the present Congregational Church, the Catholic Church in Poquonock and the former Baptist Church of Rainbow illustrate the fact that the religious life of a community is influenced greatly by the business life.

We have noticed that the first two meeting-houses were in the section called Elm Grove. Here the majority of the people lived. The stores, early mill, blacksmith shop, school, postoffice, hotel and social hall were built.

Poquonock, being situated on the Farmington River, became an Industrial Community. Mills were built near the river in Rainbow two miles north and at Eels Harbor about one mile north of Elm Grove. Eels Harbor became a legal port of entry. Elderly people can remember large ships coming to the Harbor. Many of the first people who came to work in the mills were Scotch or English. Being for the most part strict Scotch Presbyterians the Universalist services at Elm Grove did not appeal to them. Orthodox preaching services were started in a chapel[1] at Rainbow in 1835. Rev. David A. Sherman was the first minister who held services there. Later students from the Theological Institute at East Windsor[1] supplied the pulpit. Rev. Mr. Hempstead of Hartford preached in Rainbow from the spring of 1840 to that of 1841. During his ministry there was a revival. We read from a letter written by a former inhabitant:

> "There has not been many balls here for the year past, we are getting to be very good. We have had something of a revival of Religion here among the Presbyterians; they have formed a Church[2] and have about forty members a great part of them belong in Rainbow."[3]

Mr. Hempstead was succeeded by Rev. John R. Adams who held services at the schoolhouse in Poquonock Center. During Rev. Mr. Adams ministry the Church was organized. The council met in the

---

[1] Building stood until a few years ago across the road from the home of Mr. and Mrs. Frank E. Clark. Building was used at various times by the Catholics and the Baptists also.

[1] Theological Institute at East Windsor now the Hartford Theological Seminary.

[2] The church was organized as a Congregational Church. There was a very close connection between the early Congregational and Presbyterian churches.

[3] .Letter, Poquonock, Conn., August 15, 1841. In possession of the writer. (last page missing).

old meeting-house June 2, 1841 to consider organizing the Church. The articles of faith and the covenant adopted by the newly organized group were approved of by the council. The Church was then duly organized as the Second Church in Windsor.

The service was as follows:

"Introductory Prayer, Rev. Mr. Hemenway.
Sermon   Rev. Dr. Hawes.
Reading Articles of faith and administration of baptism to candidates, Rev. Mr. Adams.
Consecration prayer, Rev. Mr. McLeon.
Fellowship of the Churches, Rev. Mr. Jewett.
Administration of the Lord's Supper,
                Rev. Mr. Bushnell and Rev. Mr. Washburn."[1]

Rev. Mr. Adams preached to the newly organized church until Oct. 31, 1841. The church was next supplied by Rev. Chauncey Rice. Like the majority of the early ministers of Poquonock, he stayed only a short time leaving on Feb. 13, 1842.

Rev. Cornelius B. Everest became the next pastor. The church at this time met in the Chapel at Rainbow. During the last two years and a half of his ministry services were also held at Poquonock in a Hall[2] built for Church purposes by Mr. Daniel Buck. Rev. Mr. Bruce also preached in Poquonock at Franklin Hall sometime in 1849.

One Sunday Mr. Thomas H. Rouse from the church at Feeding-Hills exchanged with Mr. Bruce. The Poquonock people enjoyed the service so much that arrangements were made by him to preach in Poquonock regularly. For the next two years he preached to the group in Poquonock which was not organized as a church. In 1852 the group at Poquonock united with the church at Rainbow. Mr. Rouse was invited to become their pastor.

The people were soon discussing the possibility of building a church building. There were two organizations mainly responsible for the building of the church, the Ecclesiastical Society and the Female Charitable Society.

A meeting was held in Franklin Hall March 28, 1853 to consider forming a new Ecclesiastical Society[1] and to take measures for building a church edifice. The building committee was authorized to spend forty-eight hundred dollars for building the church edifice.

---

[1] Bonney, Rev. Nathaniel G., Historical Manual of the Congregational Church, Poquonock, Connecticut, p. 27 and 28, Hartford, Conn., Case, Lockwood and Brainard.
[2] It is not known definitely whether this was Franklin Hall or another building.
[1] Ecclesiastical Society named Poquonock Congregational Society.

The women in the community were soon organized to raise money for the new church. Miss Clarissa Hatheway was among the first to express the desire for a church edifice. She pledged about twenty-four dollars to the Sewing Society upon the condition that all their efforts be used for a new church.

On July 26th, 1841 the Female Charitable Society[2] was organized. Article three of the Constitution read:

"The avails of this Society shall be devoted to the purchase of Sacramental Vessels for the use of 2nd Church in Windsor, for the library of the Sabboth School in connection with said church, or for any other object as the majority shall decide at any annual meeting."[3]

The ladies raised money by sewing and by festivals. A few of the accounts read:

"An Account of work done in the Society commencing August 5th, 1842.

Sold to Mrs. Squares two needlebooks	29cts.
Repairing shirts for C. P. Clark	25cts.
Work done for Mrs. Fanny Griffin	25cts."[4]

The first record of money spent is in 1841.

"Hartford, July 25th, 1841

Mr. John B. Adams.
For the Ladies Society Poquonock.
Bought of W. H. Boardman.

1 Flaggon	$5.00
4 Goblets	5.00
2 Platters	2.00
1 Baptisimal Font	2.25
	14.25
	25
	14.00

Received Payment
W. A. Boardman."[1]

The group supported financially the Sabbath School, the Sabbath School Library and the Singing School.

After several years of hard work the present church edifice was built. The group which had wandered about from the meeting-house at Elm Grove to the schoolhouse, then to a Chapel in Rainbow and still later to Franklin Hall finally ceased their wandering. The church was dedicated April 12, 1854.

---

[2] Female Charitable Society. It is possible that this is the Sewing Society.
[3] Records of Female Charitable Society of 2nd Parish in Windsor.
[4] Ibid.
[1] Records of Female Charitable Society of 2nd Parish in Windsor.

51

B. *Second Period 1854-1889*

Soon after the church was dedicated Mr. Rouse was ordained and installed as the pastor. Two years later he accepted a call from the Congregational Church in Jamestown, New York. During his ministry in Poquonock thirty-nine people joined the church.

Rev. Henry J. Lamb was next called to the pastorate of the church. Owing to his ill health he declined to be installed. He supplied the pulpit for two years. There was a revival and fourteen joined the church on July 4, 1858.

Rev. Ogden Hall was the next pastor. After he left Rev. Charles H. Bissell, a student at the Theological Institute in East Windsor, became the acting-pastor. He was ordained as an Evangelist June 12, 1862.

He wrote of his work in Poquonock:

"Of the fruits of my pastorate at Poquonock, I cannot name anything very marked. It lingers in my mind as a very pleasant experience, with a remarkable friendly and generous people, in fact the most social and liberal with whom it has been my lot to become acquainted, either in the ministry or out of it.

_____ _____ we had no revival properly so termed, though during the winter of '61 and '62 there was a very deep state of religious feeling, and some hopeful conversions—that I have often looked back to that time with the thought that the want of experience and courage on my part prevented a glorious work of grace."[1]

The pulpit was next supplied by Rev. Josiah Peabody, a returned missionary from Turkey. He preached in Poquonock from 1865 to 1868.

On July 1, 1868 the Rev. Nathaniel G. Bonney started his ministry in Poquonock. The church celebrated its thirtieth anniversary while he was the pastor. A Church Manual was published which contained a historical sketch of the church. The hours of church services were changed from morning and afternoon to morning and evening. The Sunday School continued to grow in numbers and the Ladies had an active society.

The next few years Poquonock was at its height. There were three mills running in Rainbow and three at Poquonock Center. The majority of the people in the community were Protestants. The English and Scotch people who worked in the mills were very ardent church workers. Church attendance was so large that it was hard to get a pew. The pews were sold every year at auction.

---

[1] Bonney, Rev. N. G., Historical Church Manual Poquonock Conn., p. 34, Hartford, Conn., Case, Lockwood and Brainard, 1873.

The price paid was called "slip rent". Every person was responsible for carpeting his own pew. This plan worked very well as long as every one was able to buy the same pew the next year. The difficulty came when two people wanted the same pew. On several occasions when a person saw his pew sold to another person he would become angry and tear up the carpet. A large number of people came down from Rainbow in large busses. The social life was not forgotten. Festivals, concerts and parties were held frequently.

The next pastor Rev. Silas Ketchum was installed on Thursday, May 1, 1879. A few copies (twenty-five) of the program were printed. One day Rev. Mr. Ketchum made the remark that any boy could get an education if he wanted to. Samuel Rose, an English boy who worked in the mill, had an interview with him after hearing the remark. Rev. Mr. Ketchum became interested in the boy and tutored him. Several years later the boy decided to become a minister. Although he was doing missionary work in Georgia at the time he came back to Poquonock to be ordained as an Evangelist (October 25, 1887). The Missionary Society showed their interest in his missionary work by sending a contribution to his church in Provo, Utah.

Rev. Mr. Ketchum died, April 24, 1880 in Boston. In 1880 Rev. William H. Howard became the pastor and remained two years (1880-1882).

On June 27, 1882 Rev. Charles H. Pettibone was ordained to the ministry and was installed as pastor. He is remembered as a very friendly person well liked and extremely interested in the Young People. Some people still thought that the minister should not enter into the social life of the people. He was greatly criticized for playing baseball with the boys. If the people who criticized his playing ball had known that the Young People danced in the parsonage after Prayer meeting there certainly would have been trouble.

The Sunday evening services were well attended. They were mainly for young people. At first there was usually singing. The Moody and Sankey Gospel Songs were popular. Rev. Mr. Pettibone gave a talk, then the people had an opportunity to take part in the program.

The boys and girls gave plays and concerts. One play given was about David and Goliath. The killing of the giant was done in the vestibule, the audience only hearing a loud noise. Young David then came in proudly bringing the giant's head.

The Sunday School gave a concert every month. Singing School was also very popular at this time. Christmas was a very happy time. There was a Christmas tree at the church and presents for all the pupils.

Great importance was placed upon the memorizing of Bible verses. A record was kept of the number of verses each one learned. The Sunday School Superintendent offered a gold dollar to each one who learned a Bible verse every Sunday. A five dollar gold piece was given if they recited all the verses at the end of the year. Much to the suprise about seventeen won five dollars and twenty-two won one dollar.

The records show that the boys and girls were very much interested in missions. Mr. Duncan often told them missionary stories. A missionary concert was given every month. Talks on missions were also at the Sunday evening services. A mission circle called the Cheerful Givers was organized. This was similar to an earlier organization called the Willing Workers.

C. *Third Period 1889-1922*

1. *Ministry of Rev. Nathan T. Merwin.*   During the ministry of Rev. Nathan T. Merwin two organizations were started which played an important part in the religious life of the community.

The Women's Missionary Society was organized by Mrs. Merwin. When a prominent woman in the church heard of the new organization she said, "But Mrs. Merwin the women won't come, you can't hold regular meetings".[1] Mrs. Merwin replied, "Oh yes we can for my two daughters and myself will be there".[2] The women did come to the meetings and soon were studying about the various mission fields and contributing to them.

The Home Department was the result of a Sunday School Conference Miss Clara Hatheway attended and heard about the Home Departments of organizations in other towns. She returned from the conference determined to organize one in Poquonock. Miss Hatheway was often seen visiting her class. Soon her class of shut-ins and people who lived far from church grew until it numbered over twenty-five. At first it was feared that her work would keep people away from church but soon it was realized that she was supplementing and not competing with the regular church services. A lady living in Southbridge, Massachusetts heard about

---

[1] Letter sent to writer from Mrs. Nathalia P. M. Case, March 10, 1936.
[2] Ibid.

the class and became a member. She also helped with the cradle roll taking pictures and lesson papers to the homes where the small children lived. This group numbered about twenty.

The Ladies Benevolence Society as early as 1892 started a fund for an organ. This group raised a great deal of money for the church by fairs, festivals and plays.

Religious services were started again in the Elm Grove Chapel. The Universalist Society apparently were not having services and the people with few exceptions were not attending any church service. This section was often spoken of as "the barren waste". Rev. Mr. Merwin started preaching services in the Elm Grove Chapel in the summer of 1894. There is a report at the Congregational House in Hartford which states:

> "Mr. Merwin visits the Universalists and Spiritualists in the vicinity of the cemetery chapel and hopes to win them to the truth. Mrs. Thrall, a spiritualist physician in that vicinity has a large practice."[1]

The services were enjoyed very much. Some one suggested that as long as Mr. Merwin had services only two Sunday afternoons a month in the Chapel that someone else supply the other Sundays. At this time a Trinity College student, Mr. Karl Reiland was conducting services in Bloomfield. Someone suggested that the group have him at Elm Grove when Mr. Merwin did not have the service.

For several weeks the Chapel was filled. The young people especially enjoyed the services and the Trinity student was popular with all the people. All went well until the services were stopped very suddenly as the minister of the Windsor Episcopal Church reminded them of the ruling[1] in the Episcopal Church concerning several Episcopal services in the same town. The people who were responsible for having the services did not realize that Poquonock was in the town of Windsor. Then too, they did not consider them as church services. Mr. Reiland was not an ordained minister at this time. Although a letter of protest was sent to the Bishop when the services were stopped services were never started again. The money collected by the group for hymn books was given to a widow who lived near by. The organ loaned by the Baptists may still be in the Chapel. The services conducted by Rev. Mr. Merwin were discontinued. This was the last attempt at having religious services in the Elm Grove section.

No signature, report dated June 25, 1894, Congregational House, 37 Garden Street, Hartford, Conn.

There is a ruling that two Episcopal services cannot be held in the same town without permission of the first church.

2. *Ministry of Rev. William C. Prentiss (1898-1902).* Rev. William C. Prentiss came to the Poquonock Church directly from the Hartford Theological Seminary. He was ordained in the Church.

In writing of the people who made up the community he says:

"In my day, there were two quite different influences in the parish which contributed to the cosmopolitan character of this community extending from the Farmington valley from the Windsor border on the south to the Granby boundry on the north. In Rainbow there was still in existence, as I remember, a small Baptist Church. But much of the time these loyal, devoted people worshiped at Poquonock and assisted in the maintenance of the church life. In their religious life, they were men and women with strong, personal convictions, and devoted and consecrated in Christian service. These people with their fine, Christian spirit, helped to deepen the spiritual life of the church and also gave an added breadth of outlook to the church."[1]

Later on he writes:

"The other influence existed mostly in the Southern part of the town, resulting from an old spiritualist society. I think that this organization was in existence when I first came to Poquonock. My pastoral work extended to these homes where I found appreciation and loyalty and where my ministries seemed accep-able. In the affairs of the community, in which I sometimes had a part, there was no lack of cooperation, and many of my best friends lived in these homes in which I was always welcomed. There was, however, a subtile influence which I seem to feel at times when trying to enlist the young people in the church and when endeavoring to bring the older people of this part of the community into the more distinctive religious life."[2]

During his ministry the organ was dedicated Oct. 19, 1900. From a church calendar we know that the church had the following organizations: Ladies' Helpers, Sunday School, Christian Endeavor, Ladies Benevolence Society, Cheerful Givers, Woman's Missionary Society and King's Daughter.

Three organizations were started during his ministry. The first was a boy's club. The boys secured a printing press. They printed the programs, tickets, and calendars. A boy's camp was also started, it being the first one on the Farmington River.

A Good Citizenship Club was organized at the parsonage October 7, 1901. The purpose of the club is stated in Section Two,

---

[1], [2] Report sent to writer from Rev. William C. Prentiss, March 12, 1936.

Article I of the Constitution:

"The object of this club shall be to promote Good Citizenship, and to arouse active action for good government by a discussion of Current Issues."[1]

Some of the papers read at the meetings were The Constitutional Convention, Growth of Cities, Christ and Social Problems. Some of the topics of debate were: (1) the Philippines should be given their independence, (2) The President was indiscreet in inviting a colored man to dine with him. The last meeting recorded is March 18, 1902.

There were many socials and concerts held. The Punch and Judy shows and the giant bat made by Mr. C. Robert Hatheway are still remembered. The Annual Harvest Festival as usual was an enjoyable occasion. As in former years the women added not only to the social life but to the church treasury by the many fairs and church suppers held.

The more religious life of the people was met by the four services on Sunday, the Prayer Meeting, the Pastor's Class and the Annual Week of Prayer.

3. *Ministry of Rev. Edward O. Grisbrook.* Rev. William C. Prentiss left Poquonock in March, 1902. The church was without a pastor until October 1902. During this period here was a lessening in church activities. June 5, 1902 a Poquonock girl wrote home,

"I can just see us in about five years from now in the Windsor Church. Can't you? I can't imagine there being any church at Poquonock at least any interesting one."[1]

Although many of the church people were discouraged, soon the church organizations were revived and built up. The men in the church were interested in fixing up the church barn to be used as a boy's club room. It was open every evening as a reading and game room.

The church became the social center for the Protestants in the community. Husking bees, fairs, church suppers, an Old Maid's Convention, and plays added a large sum of money to the treasury as well as being enjoyed immensely.

Secretary's Book Good Citizenship Club. Loaned by Mr. Charles H. Schneiler.

Letter June 5, 1902 from Miss Carrie P. Marshall to Mrs. David E. Marshall. n possession of writer.

The growing spirit of tolerance and cooperation between the various groups is emphasized in a letter written by the pastor who writes of his work in Poquonock:

"While I was there I endeavored and succeeded a good deal in breaking down a feeling of estrangement that existed between the more definite church people and a group that were known as Spiritualists, by visiting with them and developing among the church people a broadmindedness and more tolerant spirit. They came occasionally to the morning service of worship, assisted in the financial matters, and participated in the social life of the church."[1]

The fine spirit which already existed between the Baptists and the Congregationalists is shown in a letter from a Baptist who writes,

"Tonight is the church roll call. Of course none of us are members of this church but because we go here and are members elsewhere we have invitations and expect to go."[2]

The number of Protestants in Poquonock was decreasing. Rev. Mr. Grisbrook in recalling the people of Poquonock writes:

"There is one thing that stands out in my memory and that is the aggressive, daring faith and devotion of a few people, determined in face of a dwindling Protestant population to keep the church going strong, nothing was too laborious to undertake and with enthusiasm they put things across. It was surprising to me. As I look back over my pastorates I can see standing out in each something that has helped me to become a better minister. Poquonock taught me to venture and believe that what seemed impossible could be done."[1]

4. *Ministry of Rev. William Carr.* Rev. William Carr became the pastor of the church October 24, 1907. The church at the time was noted for its fine social activities. The Strawberry Festival and the Chicken Pie Suppers attracted much attention. They were attended by both the Catholics and Protestants.

One of the Christmas parties was especially enjoyed. For many years Poquonock had had an annual Christmas party, but one year the children were especially favored by having Mr. and Mrs. Santa Claus come to the church in a real sleigh.

The vestry of the church was often used for Farm Bureau meetings. The Missionary Society and the Benevolence Society have

---

[1] Letter sent to writer from Rev. E. O. Grisbrook, Jan., 15, 1936.
[2] Letter, Dec. 15, 1902, from Mrs. Bertha H. P. Rogers to Miss Carrie P Marshall. In possession of writer.
[1] Letter, January 15, 1936, to writer from Rev. E. O. Grisbrook.

lways had many fine speakers on their programs. The Benevo-ence Society continued to be one of the main financial supports f the church.

The Young People took an active part in the Christian Endeavor vork. They attended the conferences held in various churches and ne of their members attended the World's Christian Endeavor Jonvention held in New York City in 1921.

In 1912 the electric equipment was installed in the church. It vas given as a Christmas present by Rev. N. T. Merwin and Mr. nd Mrs. Fredus Case in memory of Mrs. N. T. Merwin and "Baby Jase, Little Love Bird".

Later in 1915 the parsonage was wired, the money being given y a class of girls who called themselves the S.P.I.

Attendance at church services was gradually decreasing. The Jhurch, however, during this period was very active socially and vas very missionary-minded. The Sunday School, Christian En-eavor and Missionary Society all contributed liberally to missions.

D. *Fourth Period 1922-1936*

Rev. Victor L. Greenwood, pastor

We have noticed a growing spirit of tolerance and appreciation mong the various religious groups in the community. One of the utstanding expressions of this spirit is shown in the reorganiza-on of the Poquonock Congregational Church to form the Poquon-ck Community (Congregational) Church Incorporated.

The Ecclesiastical Society disbanded June 21, 1924 and turned ie church property over to the church. The requirements for lurch membership were changed making it unnecessary to sign denominational creed. The following letter was sent to the Pro-stants in the community:

Poquonock, Conn., March 6, 1924

"Dear Friend:

Our Poquonock Community Church has gone beyond the ex-perimental stage.

Usually a new minister in a Church means a short season of curiosity and enthusiasm with a return of old members who have lost interest. The season soon passes and once more the Church marks time. Outside of this small circle there is always the larger circle of folks who live on unmoved by the work of the Church. We feel that this whole Community is definitely com-mitted to the support of a Christian Fellowship that shall enthuse and inspire every man, woman and child in our midst.

Now a Community Church is the whole Community in fellowship for more brotherly living. It does not presume to dictate to the Community. It finds out the needs of the Community and seeks to meet them.

A Community Church seeks to express religion in a way so simple and at the same time so fundamental that every resident may feel at home in its fellowship. Religion is just friendship. Friendship with Father God and friendship with Brother Man.

All of us Protestants in this Parish want to feel that we are members one with another in the conscious love of Father God and Brother Man.

Our Community Church is not going to apologize for seeking to interest every individual in a way of living that shall make happier folks, happier homes and a happier Community.

Our Community Church is not looking upon its minister as an official to be called on only in times of crisis, or as a necessary ornament valuable or otherwise to the town, or as one whose public prayers and preaching shall take folks to Heaven by proxy. This whole Community through its Community Church, is looking upon its ministers as a friend, brother and adviser who shall serve the Community by sensing its needs and enthusing all folks here to meet these needs and solve its problems in the spirit of the Master of us all.

This will mean as time goes on a Community so knit together by fellowship and service that folks here now will never want to live elsewhere, and folks elsewhere will want to come and live here in this homelike atmosphere.

We think the time has come when all folks in our Community should be given a chance to join hands.

Of course you understand for good reasons the majority of folks in our Community feel that our Church should still be affiliated with the Congregational Denomination. But note carefully that this does not mean any control from outside our Parish.

As Dr. W. E. Barton says:

'You are not required to become a Congregationalist in order to unite with a Congregational church. A Congregational church is not a church of Congregationalists, but a church of Christians in which the congregation governs. It has absolutely no sectarian tests. To belong to a Baptist church one must be a Baptist, submitting to a particular rite administered in a particular form. To belong to an Episcopal church one must be an Episcopalian. Congregationalism has no such divisive tests.'

Therefore in joining hands, we join hands as a group of Christians, for deeper friendship and fellowship. We join hands or no creed but as a basis of fellowship we think the following is all that is necessary for folks to assent to:

Having become vitally conscious of the saving power of my personal fellowship with Father God and Brother Man, I desire to unite with the members of this Community Church, that I may the more effectively further the cause of truth, righteousness and love.

The date for joining hands in this our fellowship has been set for Sunday morning, April 13, the Sunday before Easter.

Those who have been members of the Church here will on that date, by rising, give assent to the above desire, and thus join hands with the larger fellowship. Those who have not been members and desire to join hands on the above basis will then rise and the minister will lead in prayer asking our Father's blessing on this union of Christians for the furtherance of fellowship and service in our Community.

This must be a co-operative effort, for the minister cannot possibly do all the personal work required. To this end will all men who desire this union hand their names to Mr. Charles A. Huntingdon? Will all women hand their names to Mrs. R. A. Hagarty?

The minister is meeting the Young People of the Parish Tuesday Evenings during March at 7:30 P. M. in the Vestry of the Church.

If singly or in groups, any of the men or women of the Parish wish to consult the minister he will willingly respond.

One word more. Do not think this is only for the other fellow. Consider thoughtfully all that the above means to yourself and your community and let us all together put our beloved Church on a strong, sane co-operative basis that shall insure its constructive development through all the years to come.

Most cordially and fraternally,

VICTOR L. GREENWOOD."[1]

A growing appreciation of people of other creeds and races has been developed. This has been done in several ways. The Missionary Society has speakers from other countries. A Hindu student has not only spoken at Young People's Meeting but also at the Sunday Morning Service. Jewish people have added to the Easter service by their music.

One of the first series of events which brought the Community into cantact with the Church was the Communiy Sunday Evening programs. These were conducted for seven years. The first part of the program was a worship service conducted by the minister. The worship service was followed by a social hour of moving pictures.

The latest project is that of improving the Church grounds. A few years ago some students in the Hartford School of Religious

Greenwood, Victor L, Letter sent to Protestants in the Community of Poonock, March 6, 1924.

Education made plans for improving the Church grounds. These were presented to the Church and helped to arouse interest in the Church grounds.

The minister had for many years dreamed of improving the Church grounds. After consultation with a horticulturalist work started in 1934. The men worked very hard and soon the yard was greatly improved. The pictures taken in 1934 and 1935 illustrate what can be done in a short time when a group is willing to work hard. The plan of improving the Church lawn and edifice is arranged in Units of Work. It is hoped that all the Units will be completed by 1941.

It is not the purpose of this paper to make a careful critical examination of the present church organization but rather to point out the main factors which have influenced the religious life of the community.

Although the present church is influenced by the past, new problems are constantly arising which must be met.

"New occasions teach new duties; time makes Ancient good uncouth.

"They must upward still and onward, who would keep abreast of Truth."[1]

---

[1] Lowell, James Russell, The Present Crisis.

EARLIEST ACCOUNTS OF THE SOCIETY

The early Ecclesiastical Society Records of Poquonock are lost. We have, however, an eighteen page document which tells about the building of the church and the method of supporting the church. The following is a copy of the document. There are a few illegible words. In these cases a _____ line is made. The spelling is as in the original.

Page one.

"June, 1726.

The Society debtor to Benjamin Smith, by seventeen bushel of lime,	£I	18	0
Will. Phelpsis account warning meeting,	0	02	6
By going after Mr. Woodbridge,	0	05	0
By entertaining Mr. Woodbridge three Sabbaths	0	07	6
By entertaining Mr. Woodbridge ten weeks,	3	10	0
By keeping Mr. Woodbridge's hor(se) four weeks,	0	06	6
John Phelpsis account by money disbursed a going after Mr. Woodbridge,	0	01	6
Joseph Pinney, for warning a meeting,	0	02	6
November 13, 1727.			
Samuel Phelpsis account by warning two meetings,	0	05	0
By half hundred of b(oar)ds,	0	03	0
To Corneliun Brown for going to Weathersfield and other services,	0	06	0

Ordered to Benjamin More nine shillings and ten pence. to Cornelius Brown four shillings for his going after the Rev. Ministry to ordain Mr. Woodbridge."

Page two.

March 1827 Sosiaty Debter.

"To Daniel Phelps for warning a meeting,	0	2	10
To Daniel Griswold for three day works him and hors[1] for fixing and copey of Court act,		14	8
To Isac Gilet for putting up windows and glass and making 1100 window frams	0	14	0
The Society is indetd John Owen the sum of one pound - nineteen shillings	1	19	0
John Owen by order for this one pound nineteer _____.			

Page three.

"May 1727.

The Sosiaty debtor to Josheph Barnard by seevn days tendance at cour[1] and money paid in Joseph Barnard

paid to Mr. Fuller	2	3	0
paid to Mr. Fuller	0	11	6
insign George Griswold	1	00	0
Sargant Benjamin Griswold	1	0	0
Sariant Benajah Holcomb	0	30	0
William Cluck	0	40	0
John Owen	1	00	0
Sariant John Griswold	0	80	0
Maxiah Pinney	0	6	0
Wido holcomb[2]	0	13	0
Nathaniel Griswold	0	6	0
Ephriam Phelps	0	10	0
Frances Griswold	0	15	0
Cernelas phelps	11	05	0
David Marshall	0	13	6
Josheph holcomb	0	10	0
John Griswold for a writ to get the rate	0	2	0
Nathel Griswold money paid to mother at Court 3 days	00	08	0

Page four

"Reveived of Thomas Griswold December ye 1728 the some of one hundred and four pound fifteen shilling and five pence

104	10	0
5	10	0
110	06	0

"Ordered Thomas Griswold to pay to Mr. Woodbrig[1] the som of _____ pound eight shillings and six pence.

80	00	0

Thomas Griswold has pay of the above order the sum of five pounds and _____ shillings as appears by his resait[2] dated July 3rd, 1730.

44	16	8

frances guswold and William phelps 2 are Detor for a rate delivered to them by the Commit[3] sum of eighty pounds.

Mr. John Woodbridg	10	00	0
Mr. John Woodbridg	07	00	0
Mr. John Woodbridg	08	00	0
Mr. John Woodbridg	07	10	0
	32	10	
	4		
	36	10	
What money together	120	8	2

---

[1] seevn days tendance at court—seven days attendance at court.
[2] wido holcomb—Widow Holcomb.
[1] Mr. Woodbrig—Mr. Woodbridge.
[2] resait—receipt.
[3] Commit—Committee.

Page five.

"Feb. 19, 1729.

The commety have alowed as folers[4] to ＿＿＿ men as folers for work don[5] to the meeting hous.[6]

To Shubok Griswold for one day's work at the met hous[7]	3	6	0
To Cornd Phelps for 3 days work and his team and son	0	16	6

Lt
Samuel Phelps one ＿＿＿

December 6, 1728.

An account of the order that the comety gave to Thomas Griswold wich[8] he has payed as apers[9] by share.

Repairs—severall men	06	02	0
To John Griswold	02	14	0
To cornellus browne	00	06	6
To thomas Griswold	15	01	9
To Severall pasons	18	13	10
To Mr. John Woodbridge	07	00	0
To John Brown and Joseph piney		01	26
To Cap Gorg Griswold	01	00	8
To John Griswold	02	16	0
To Danell phelps	00	02	10
Edward Griswold	00	12	10
John Griswold	01	01	3
John Brown Rate[1] with was given	1	00	0
To Nathanell Griswold	19	11	11
To mony pay by Thomas Griswold	07	00	3
Mon pay to severall Men	09	12	7
To Nathanal Griswold	01	00	00
To Danell Griswold	00	14	8
To Thomas Griswold	09	05	10
	114	19	8
＿＿＿ for four pound payed Mr. Woodbridge	004	00	0
	118	19	8

Page six.

"Account of the orders that the Committee gave unto John Owen, Collector which he has paid as appears by their resaits:

To Ephraim Phelps the sum of two shillings and 6,	0	02	6
Also to Obadiah Owen one shilling and six pence,	0	01	6

Folers—follows.
Don—done.
Hous—house.
Met hous—meeting-house.
Wich—which.
Apers—appearance.
Rate—amount of money to be paid to the Ecclesiastical Society towards the pport of the Church.

Also to Samuel Phelps, Jr., eight shillings	0	08	0
" Mr. John Woodbridge the sum of seven pound, ten,	7	10	-0
Also to Benj. Griswold, Jr., the sum of four pound 19,	4	19	0
Also to John Owen one pound,	1	00	0
" Ephraim Phelps the sum of ten shillings,	0	10	0
Also to Benj. Griswold one pound,	1	00	0
" Obadiah Owen fourteen shillings and six,	0	14	6
Also to Noadiah Gillet, fifteen shillings	0	15	0
" Thomas Phelps nine shillings,	0	09	0
Also John Griswold, Comttman, rec'd	3	00	0
To Benj. Griswold, Jr., one pound, 11 shillings 8,	1	11	8
" Isaac Gillet fourteen shillings,	0	14	0
To Mr. Woodbridge by John Owen,	4	00	00
" Mr. Woodbridge by John Owen,	3	13	00
" Noadiah Gillet,	0	05	00
	£30	13	2

Dec. 6, 1728, Thomas Griswold was ordered 'to pay to Mr. Woodbridge the sum of seven pound, eight shillings and six pence.' 'Thomas Griswold has paid of this above order the sum of five pound and ten shillings, as appears by his resait, dated July 3d, 1730.'

Page seven.

"May 7th, 1729 then received of Society Committee ye full _____ of twenty four pound shillings on ye account of ye money. Due to me from ye Society— pay by ......

Jon Woodbridge.

October 28, 1730 Yn Received of Ye Society committee ye sum of one hundred and thirteen pounds nine shillings and three pence—Received per me.

Jon Woodbridge.

Page eight.

"Nathanell peney from county. allowed aprall 12,[1] 1729 for going to harford with John Owen	0	04	0
Mor for going to harford to tak out Thrall will	0	04	0
Mor for three copye[2]	0	02	0
Mor for going to Torkey hils[3]	0	04	0
Mor for going over the grat river[4] and __ing	0	05	0
Mor for keeping Woodbridges horse	0	01	0

My account order _____ by the collector
To the above named Nathanal peney _____

---

[1] Aprall—April.
[2] Copye—Copies.
[3] Torkey hils—Turkey Hill (now East Granby).
[4] Grat river—Great River—Connecticut.

Wheir as Nathanell peney ⎯⎯ has made appear to the Lystors[5] of the year 1728 that he was overcharged in ⎯⎯ list the sum of ten pound of payable estate wich was on over rate seven and nine pence ⎯⎯ rate for it was made ⎯⎯ peney per pound.

Jannry 16, 1730, then Received of Gorg Nath peney collector the sum of one hundred twenty six pound six shilling and six peney.

On ye account by rate he was to gather of the Society.

Page nine.

"David Marshall account alowed April 22, 1729.

for nine shilling and six pence pay to Na-thanell Griswold	0	9	0
for going over the great river and measuring	0	5	0
Mor for going to Cap Moore ⎯⎯	0	1	0
Mor for going to harford to Cort	0	4	0
Mor for four shillings payed Noah Peney	0	4	0

Sept. 1735.

Then received of Nathaniel pinny collector one pound three shillings and eight pence and two pounds and one shilling all	3	4	8

Page ten.

May 9, 1729—Then recd of the Society a rate. The sum of a hundred and seventy five pounds together of the Third or West Society[1] and to deliver to the sI Comity[2] I say recd by me Daniel Griswold Colector.

Credit of Danell Griswold has payed to severall pasons.

To Mr John Woodbridge ye sum of	129	13	0
To Samuel Phelps	002	01	
To Daniel Griswold ⎯⎯	1	12	0
To William Barber ⎯⎯	0	13	0
To Peletiah Griswold	0	2	6
To Cap Gorge Griswold	0	17	0
Ye comtee ⎯⎯	1	10	9
	124	9	3

Page eleven.

May 19, 1729.

"Account of the orders that the Comety gave to Daniel ⎯⎯ colector to pay ⎯⎯ ⎯⎯ pasons the severall sums annexed to thar ⎯⎯ ⎯⎯ Mr. John Woodbridg

To Shubal Gris' order given out for	155	00	0
To Cornell phelps ⎯⎯	0	16	6
Taxing Saml phelps	2	01	00
⎯⎯ William phelps	1	01	09

[5] Lystors—Listers (people who made out the tax list.)
[1] Called West to distinguish from society of East Windsor.
[2] SI Comity—Said Committee.

To David phelps _____	0	03	6
to Granny Griswold _____	0	14	0
To Mathew Griswold _____	0	02	6
To Co_____ Brown _____	0	07	6
To Joseph barnard _____	7	08	0
To Zeacheas Griswold	1	11	4
To Danell Griswold	1	07	0
To Joseph phelps _____	0	10	0
To _____ phelps	0	10	0
To _____ phelps	0	19	0
To William Barber _____	0	13	0
To Danill Gillet	0	10	6
To benjaman barbur	0	13	0
To Nathanell peney junor	1	0	6
To Pelebeah Gr _____	(?)1	2	6
To Danell Griswold	0	3	6
To David Marshall	1	x3	0
To Joseph Barnard	0	11	0
To Capt. Gorge Griswold	0	17	0

Page twelve.

Feb. 14, 1728.

"The socity is indeted to severall men as folers

To Ensign Samuell phelps for warning a society meeting	0	2	6
To pellitiah griswold for warning a society meeting	0	2	6
To Will Barbur for warning an for make rate	0	5	0
To S_____ Joseph barnard for going to harford			
To S_____ Joseph barnard for keeping 11 horses one day	0	5	0
To Danell Griswold for keeping —— and measuring land	0	0	36
To David marshall for going	0	05	0
Aprall 11, 1729 the socity _____ to Nathll Griswold three pound	3	0	0

The Socity has payed this three pound to John Owen for Richard Griswold, Hartford this account is avoid.

Aprall ye 11 1729

I Nathll Griswold promiss to deliver and acquit ye society of all my Dues on ye payment of the Above Mentioned Sum _____ three pounds   03   00   0

allso to acquit ye indemnifing bonds in ye behalf of ye society of Ensign George Griswold and Joseph Barnard and Ephram Phelps and David Marshal and _____ Griswold _____ to Nathll

Griswd _____ to Nathll Griswo _____
_____ as witness our hands Nathll Griswold.

Page thirteen.

—— 17 ——

"The severall pasons acount of what Thay demand the
Socity ——

Ens Samll phelps for going to harford	0	12	0
Three days ——	0	12	0
Nor for one days of his, son and team	0	06	0
Mor for two days work and 312 feets of bords	1	00	6
Shubal Griswold acount for one days work ——	0	3	6
Cornellus phelps acount three days work	0	10	6
Mor for his son and teem[1] one day	0	06	0
Nathanell pinney account payed to John ——			
for —— 14— 6 and my work at the smithy	30	17	6
Mor for going after Mr. —— and going to ——	0	8	6
Mor to mony payed for—14-9 to —— ——	0	0	5
Mor ½ pound of —— six penny and more			
nails	0	1	0
Mor for days work with my teem	0	6	0
Mor for one day work ——	0	3	6
The received of Cap Marsll to and of —— ——	9	15	0
For Willm phelps account one day of his son			
and teem	0	6	0
Mor for —— days sho— work	0	15	9
David phelps acount one days work	0	3	0
Willm barbur acount one days work	0	3	6
Mor for making two rates	0	0	6
Capt griswold acount for four days work	0	14	0
Mathew Griswold acount to mony	0	0	5
Mor for bords for the pulpit	0	2	6
Corn— Griswold acount one days work	0	3	6

Page fourteen.

For Jpseph Barnards acount for boarding Mr. Abit			
Six weeks at six shiling ye week			
Mor for 304 feets of bords mor for lumber for	1	16	0
payed by ——	0	12.	0
Teachary Grisw— account for 505 feets of			
bords at the hundred ——	1	4	0
he has reseved mony fruit and eaight pinc	0	5	8
Danell Grisd —— acount for goin to Samon brook[1] after bords			
Mor for one days carting bords	0	3	6
Mor for mony payed to Zecheas Gris ——	0	3	8
Mor for three days ½ work about the flore	0	5	8
and the gallary	0	12	5
Mor for going—Mr. Abit	0	2	6
Mor for —— pint and half of Romb[2]	0	3	6

[1] Teem—team of horses.
[1] Samon brook—few rods south of West Granby Post Office.
[2] Romb—Rum

Mor for a pint and gill of brandy	0	1	0
reseved of Willm phelps three shillings five peny	0	3	5
Josiah phelps for three days work	1	0	6
phelps for three days work	1	0	6
Samll phelps for four hundred bords	0	16	0
Mor for carting bords and ___	0	3	0
Benj Barbur acount for him self and teem one day	0	6	0
Mor for two days work	0	7	0
Danell Gillets acount for three days work	0	10	0
the above acount is ordered to the collector to pay to	1	73	15

Page fifteen.

___ember 12, 1729[3]. Then the Comety received of francis griswold colector thes orders as payed as appers by their r___ payed to the severall pasond the severall some annexed to their ___

To John Brown ___	1	5	0
To Ariah peney ___	1	4	0
To John Griswold ___	1	14	4
To Joseph Barnard ___	1	16	0
To David Griswld	0	16	0
To David Marshall	0	8	0
To David phelps	0	10	9
To Cornellus phelps	2	00	0
To Mathew Griswold	1	17	0
Jonathan brown	1	11	8
___ ___ Willm phelps	2	00	0
To Cor. Frances Grisold	12	00	0
	27	4	4
To Cap George Grisold	2	00	0
To Mr. Abit	0	12	7
To Nathanell peney	7	9	9
	37	6	8

Page sixteen.

"Reseved of Francis Griswold ___ the ___ 12 ___ 1729 the some of thirty seven pounds six shillings and oaught pence on the acount of a rate he gathered for the socity.

October 24, 1729 then received a orden Copt. Francis Griswold from Mr. Woodbrig for ___ Samll phelps the sum of forty shillings mor for two pound and ___ shillings

	37	6	8
	2	0	0
	2	10	0
	41	16	8

febar 2, 1729 then reseved of Willm phelps the sum of four pound ___ shillings on the acount of his rate he was to gather for the society

	4	10	0
Mor for one pound six shilling ___	1	06	0
Mor for thirty pounds	30	00	0
	35	16	0

---

[3] Page torn, no doubt means September.

Page seventeen.

"May ye 12:1727 then Davi d Marshall payd to Noah piny the
sum of four shillings for the society   0   4   0
also payed to Noah piney by Cornelas Phelps   10   0
Eph Phelps is a _____
By money paid to Noah piney   0 17   6
by warning a meeting _____   0 02   6

Page eighteen.

"March 1, 1726—then received of John on _____ one pound and
six pence on _____ rate _____   1   0   6
also payed to Nathaniel Griswold by _____   2   0   0
July 29: 1728 then received of John Owen   1   0   0
   the sum of one pound
August 5, 1728 then received of John Owen the som of
     0 10   0
Then Rec _____ with John Owen and _____
   _____ due to the _____ from him the som of
   fifteen p__ shillings and one peny   8 15 19 1

Febr. 4, 1729.
   Resev__ of John Owen the som of
Seven poun__ shilling eleven peny _____   10 11
May 19, 1729 then reseved of John Owen _____   8   8   2
Collector the some of three pound   3 13   0
May 19, 1729 these reseved of John Owen   11   3 11
Collector for the som of three   3   0   0
                      14   3 10

RECORDS CONCERNING REV. DAN FOSTER

A. *To be laid before the Committee of Consociation*
19 October, 1879

"Whether a minister, whom a people have discharged from his pastoral relation to them, by refusing or neglecting to give him a Gospel support for the time past, may, consistent with the laws and rules of the Gospel, continue his pastoral relation to them, on supposition they give him a Gospel support for the future, and make up also their past refusal or neglect?

"If this be affirmed; then,

"Secondly, Is a minister, under the given circumstances, bound by the rules of the Gospel to continue his pastoral relations or is he at liberty to act as his own inclination, judgment or wisdom shall direct him?

"If a minister may, yea, if he is obliged, by the rules of the Gospel to continue his pastoral relation, on the above supposition; how long is he bound to wait upon his people, and continue his labours with them, to see whether they will or will not make up their past neglects, and give him sufficient reason to expect a future Gospel support among them? Or, to be more direct, if the Pastor of the 2nd Church of Christ in Windsor may, if he be bound to continue his pastoral relation to said Church on supposition the people of his charge make up their past neglect, and give him sufficient reason to expect a future Gospel support among them; how long is he bound to continue his pastoral relation to them, and wait upon his people, to see whether they will or will not comply with their duty to him as their Pastor, in the matter of his past and future support?

"Whether the Pastor of ye 2nd Church in Windsor, in his present situation, is under obligations to make any more overtures to the people of his charge, as to the matter of his temporal support?

"This venerable Council is doubtless acquainted by this time, with some of the doubts and difficulties which ly in the mind of the subscriber, concerning the continuance of his pastoral relation to the Church and people of the 2nd Society in Windsor. I mean to pay all becoming attention to the advice of wise and good men, and of this venerable Council in particular; but if my present mental difficulties are not removed, I earnestly request I may not be advised to continue my pastoral relation to this people any longer.

I am, Gentlemen, your most obedient humble servant,

DAN FOSTER"

B. Report of the Committee appointed by this Society, Mr. Foster being present March 2nd, 1780.

"Whereas heretofore some difficultys have arisen between the Reverand Dan Foster, Pastor of the 2nd Church of Christ in Windsor and the people of this Society arising as this Society suppose from some charges exhibited by said Pastor against this people and complained of at difrent times and in difrent ways which complaints we doubt hath in some degree sowered the minds of many of the good people of this Society as appears by their vote in a Society meeting on the 7th day of February last past, and as we are not striving for the Mastry but seeking peace as we hope for the sake of peace would beg leave to suggest to the said Rev. Pastor the matters at which we conclude this people have taken umbrage (and also ask of him to lend a helping hand as far as is his part to settle the same that for the future the Ordinances of the Gospel may not be neglected in this place and that empty seats in the House of God may no more witness discord between Pastor and people). The first thing we at present would mention is an absolute Charge against this Society (by letter) of breach of Covenant with our Pastor and that nothing short of our acknowledgement of breach of Covenant with him and engagement to fullfil it for the time past and to come would give him any satisfaction and also a like Charge was exhibited by the Venerable Consociation who met on the 28th day of Sept. 1779, at this place and heared and considered of the matters therein contained. Now, as soft words turn away wrath, we would in an honest and humble manner ask of our Rev. Pastor whether or no if this article of Complaint had been exhibited in softer terms it would not have been better on the whole.

21y. The second thing we would mention which we suppose gave and still gives the people of this Society some uneasiness was that article of Charge against this people respecting their Gratuitys between such a particular time and such other time as Complaint will appear—now, we may suppose from what appeared before the Consociation at other times in the year the peoples Liberality appeared conspicuous—now, we would suggest to our Rev. Pastor that we are thoughtfull of too much of a disigne was early intended against this people or else that account would not have been kept apart would never have been exhibited against us and still would have been kept more exactly which latter we hope did not happen designedly but through pure mistake arising from the peculiar circumstances of our Rev. Pastor's as it was difficult for him to know if all their Gratuitys at the time.

On Mr. Foster's personal appearance in this Meeting and by proper retraction in open Meeting hath fully satisfied our minds respecting the difficultys subsisting between the Rev. Dan Foster and this Society and we are willing and desirous that Mr. Foster be entitled to receive these moneys, grain and so voted by this Society in their meeting of the 25th day of October, 1779. Voted in the affirmative.

Report of the Committee appointed by this Society. Mr. Foster being present. March 2nd, 1780."

IBLIOGRAPHY

Books

The New England Clergy and the American Revolution, Durham, North Carolina, Duke University Press, 1928, 222p.

Commemorative Biographical Record of Hartford County, Connecticut, Chicago, Ill., J. H. Beers & Co., 1901, 1591p.

Connecticut Historical Collections, New Haven, Conn., Durrie & Peck and J. W. Warner, 1836, 560p.

or List of Congregational Ecclesiastical Societies Established in Connecticut Before Oct. 1818 with their Changes. Published by the Connecticut Historical Society, Hartford, 1913. Press of Pelton & King, Middletown, Conn., 1913,35p.

Side Glimpses From the Colonial Meeting-House, Boston, Mass., Houghton Mifflin & Co., 1894, 256p.

G. Historical Manual of the Congregational Church, Poquonock, Conn., Hartford, Conn., Press of Case, Lockwood & Brainard, 1873, 66p.

Contributions to the Ecclesiastical History of Connecticut, New Haven, Conn., William L. Kingsley, 1861, 562p.

The Settlement of the Connecticut Towns, Triple Number, Yale University Press, Published for the Tercentenary Committee, 1933, 75p.

The Literary Diary of Ezra Stiles, vol. I (1769-1776) New York, N.Y., Charles Scribners and Sons, 1901.

The Congregationalists As Seen in its Literature, New York, N. Y., Harper & Brothers, 1880, 326p.

Congregationalists in America, 44 East 14th St., New York, N. Y., J. A. Hill & Co., 1894, 552p.

Eames, Wilberforce | Early New England Catechisms, 311 Main St., Worcester, Mass., Press of Charles Hamilton, 1898, 111p.

Fergusson, E. Morris | Historic Chapters in Christian Education in America, New York, N. Y., Fleming H. Revell Co., 1935, 192p.

Fisher, William Arms | Ye Olde New England Psalm and Tunes 1620-1820, Boston Town, Oliver Ditson Company, 1930, 56p.

*Foster, Dan | Candid Examination of N a t h a n Strong's Eternal punishment consistent with infinite benevolence of G o d , Walpole, N e w Hampshire, Thomas and Thomas, 1803, 317p.

*Foster, Dan | A Short Essay on Civil Government, The Substance of Six S e r m o n s . Preached in Windsor October 1774, Near the Great Bridge, Hartford, Conn., Printed by Eben Watson, 1774.

*Foster, Isaac | A Defence of Religious Liberty, Mass. Bay Worcester, Printed by Isaiah Thomas, 1780, 192p.

Greene, M. Louise | The Development of Religious Liberty in Connecticut, Boston and New York, Houghton, Mifflin and Company, 1905, 552p.

Gregory, Rev. J. | Puritanism in the Old World and in the New, New York, N. Y., Fleming H. Revell Co., 1896, 406p.

*Hoadley, C. J. and Trumbull, J. Hammond | Colonial Records of Connecticut 1635-1776, 15 vols., Hartford, Conn., Case, Lockwood and Brainard.

Hoadley, C. J. | Records of the State of Connecticut Hartford, Conn., Case, Lockwood and Brainard, 1776-1825.

*Howard, Daniel | A New History of Old Windsor Conn., Windsor Locks, Conn., The Journal Press, 1935, 428p.

*Jackson, Samuel Macauley | The New Schaff-Herzog Encyclopedia of Religious Knowledge, Vol. IV Funk & Wagnalls Company, New York and London, 1909, 12 Volumes

Memoirs of the Late Rev. Abraham Marshall containing a Journal of the Most Interesting parts of his life, Printed for the author at Mount Zion, Hancock County, Georgia, 1824, 136p.

Source Book and Bibliographical Guide for American Church History, Monasha, Wisconsin, George Banta Publishing Co., 1921, 734p.

The Rise of Liberalism in Connecticut, 1828-1850 (Double Number) Yale University Press, New Haven, Published for the Tercentenary Committee, 1933, 34p.

Under the Constitution of 1818 (The First Decade), New Haven, Conn., Yale University Press, Published by Tercentenary Commission of the State of Connecticut. Committee on Historical, Publication, 1933, 20p.

The New England Meeting-House, New Haven, Conn., Yale University Press. Published by Tercentenary Commission of the State of Conn., Committee on Historical Publication, 1933, 34p.

History of Congregationalism Vol. V., America Vol. II, Boston, Congregational Publishing Co., 1881, 694p.

Connecticut in Transition, (1775-1818), Baltimore, Md., Williams and Wilkins Co., 1918, 471p.

The Evolution of the Common School, New Work, N. Y., The Macmillan Co., 1930, 590p.

A History of Religious Education in Connecticut, New Haven, Conn., Yale University Press, 1924, 402p.

The History of Ancient Windsor, 348 Broadway, New York, N. Y., Charles B. Norton, 1859, 922p.

The History and Geneologies of Ancient Windsor, Conn., (1635-1891) Hartford, Conn., Case, Lockwood and Brainard Co., 1891, Vol. I, 950p. Vol. II, 867p.

Trumbull, J. Hammond — The Memorial History of Hartford County, Conn. 1633-1884, Vol. I., Boston, Mass., Edward L. Osgood, Publisher, 1886, 704p.

Walker, George Leon — History of the First Church in Hartford, 1633-1883, Hartford, Conn., Brown & Gross, 1884, 503p.

Walker, Rev. George Leon — Some Aspects of the Religious Life of New England with special references to Congregationalists, New York, N. Y., Silver, Burdett & Co., 1897, 208p.

Walker, Williston — A History of the Congregational Church in the United States, New York, N. Y., Charles Scribner's Sons, 1899, 451p.

Weeden, William B. — Economic and Social History of New England 1620-1789, Vol. I, 447p. Vol. II, 517p., Boston & New York, Houghton, Mifflin & Company, 1890.

Miscellaneous - Primary Sources

Letters

Originals (except 3rd) in writer's possession.

*Case, Mrs. Nathalia P. M. — To writer March 10, 1936, from Milford, Connecticut.

*Conner, Rev. J. T. — To writer March 16, 1936 from St. Mary's Hospital, Waterbury, Connecticut.

*Greenwood, Rev. Victor L. — Sent to Protestants of Poquonock, Conn., March 6, 1924. Copy on file at Congregational House, 37 Garden Street, Hartford, Conn.

*Grisbrook, Rev. Edward O. — To writer, January 15, 1936, from Pachaug, Conn.

*Julian, Alice L. — To Miss Charlotte Phelps, Dec. 28, 1873, from Rockville, Connecticut.

*Marshall, David — To Mr. Francis Latham, New York City, Sept. 30, 1827, from Windsor, Conn.

*Marshall, Carrie P. — During years 1900-1904 to her mother.

*Phelps, Mr. Eli	Correspondence between Mr. Phelps and Rev. C. R. Moore, 1850; Rev. A. Norwood, 1852; Rev. L. A. Davis, 1858-1867.
*Prentiss, Rev. William C.	To writer March 12, 1936, from North Brookfield, Massachusetts.
*Rogers, Mrs. Bertha H. P.	To Miss Carrie P. Marshall of Windsor, Dec. 15, 1902, from Poquonock.

Manuscripts

June 1726 to Sept. 1735	First Society Records, Poquonock, Conn.
September 11, 1733	Letter to Poquonock Society from Rev. John Woodbridge.
July 22, 1738	Receipts from Nathaniel Rockwell for preaching in Poquonock Parish.
1740-1757	Samuel Tudor, 10 receipts. Preaching in 2nd Society, Windsor, Conn.
1747-1755	8 Receipts of Rates received from Poquonock people who belonged to the Church of England, signed by William Gibbs (Missionary).
March 29, 1762	Receipt by Ashabel Hatheway from Third Society, Windsor, Conn.
September 13, 1762	Receipt from Ebenezer Gould to Winsor Society of Poquonock.
June 9, 1763	Receipt form Ebenezer Gould.
Nov. 22, 1763	Warning Society Meeting, Third Society Windsor, Conn., to plan Ordination of Mr. Ambrose Collins.
Sept. 24, 1766	Society Meeting Warnings.
Nov. 13, 1769	Receipt from Mr. Church of Springfield for preaching to 2nd Society Windsor.
March 7, 1771	Warning Society Meeting to consider calling Mr. Dan Foster.
April 15, 1771	Warning of Society Meeting to make plans for ordination of Mr. Dan Foster, Windsor, Conn.
ay 14, 1771	Bill Second Society of Windsor Dr. to Thomas Griswold for refreshments served at ordination of Rev. Dan Foster, Poquonock, Conn.

January 14, 1777	Plan for having Church Services continued.
Sept. 21, 1779	Letter to Poquonock Society from Rev. Dan Foster.
January 21, 1780	Warning, 2nd Society Meeting, to discuss relationship between Rev. Dan Foster and the Poquonock Church.
Feb. 7, 1780	2nd Society, Windsor. Society not satisfied with Rev. Dan Foster.
October 19, 1779 March 2, 1780 September 15, 1799	Correspondence between Rev. Dan Foster and the North Consociation in Hartford, Conn.
October 1783	Receipt from Dan Foster to Windsor North Society.
March 22, 1788	Baptist Dissenter's Certificate. Refers to Baptist meetings in town.
1797	Manuscript from Cicero Phelps and Cyrus Phelps. Land given for Second Meeting-House at Elm Grove.
1792-1801	10 Certificates, Episcopal. Poquonock people joining Saint Andrews Episcopal Church in Simsbury, Conn.
August 9, 1800 January 1, 1804	Certificate from Baptist Dissenters.
January 1, 1808	Certificate from Methodist Dissenter.
Januaru 1, 1808	Certificate from Universalist Dissenter.
Jan 1, 1808 C	Certificate from Isaac Pinney who professed to believe in the free and independent Church of Christ.
December 1828	Copy of Patent for Rag Cutting Machine U. S. Patent Office signed by Henry Clay, Secretary of State. Richard Niles of Poquonock bought right to use the patent from Moses Y. Beach. Niles and Marshall mill was located at Elm Grove near Stony Brook.
Dec. 26, 1840	Notice of Town meeting to vote on Prohibition.
Sept. 24, 1906	Edward O. Grisbrook, Pastor's letter to church.

No date	Manuscript from Juliet Niles telling about houses in Poquonock before 1800. Original in care of Windsor Trust Co., Windsor, Conn.
No date	Slip Rent Receipt, Poquonock Congregational Society.
No date	Manuscript by Elihu Marshall telling about Post Office.
No date	Protest from Elm Grove inhabitants when Post Office was to be removed in Rainbow.
No date	Manuscript, Poquonock Union Library Constitution.
No date	Young Men's Debating Society of Poquonock, Constitution, Topics for debates.

Programs

Dec. 29, 1864	Poster, Festival given in Elm Grove Hall by Universalist Society.
July 4, 1876	Report of the Centennial Celebration of the Anniversary of our Independence at Windsor, Conn. Hartford, Conn., Case, Lockwood and Brainard Co., 1876. 48p.
1879	Program, Installation of Silas Ketchum as Pastor of The Second Congregational Church of Windsor, Conn. Windsor, Conn., Geo. C. Ketchum, printer.
June 2, 1891	Fiftieth Anniversary of the Poquonock Congregational Church.
March 1, 1907	Invitation to Reception.
September 26, 1909	Rally Day Program
1917-1918	Woman's Missionary Society, Poquonock Congregational Church.
1918-1919	Woman's Missionary Society, Poquonock Congregational Church, program for year.
Oct. 19, 1900	Dedication of the new organ, Poquonock Congregational Church.
January 23, 1901	Notice the Ladies Benevolent Society of Poquonock Congregational Church.
Feb. 13, 1901	Poster, Rummage Sale, Mr. F. M. Case, Chairman.

1902	Christian Endeavor Prayer Meeting Topics, Congregational Church.
Dec. 16, 1902	Birthday Greeting, Congregational Church Parlors.
Jan. 12, 1904	Call to a Covenant Service, Poquonock, Connecticut, Rev. Edward O. Grisbrook, pastor.
Nov. 19-26, 1905	The First Church of Christ in Windsor, Conn., 1630-1905, The Two hundred and seventy-fifth Anniversary. H a r t f o r d , Conn., Press of The Hartford Printing Co., 1906, 87p.
June 7, 1911	Advertisement of Strawberry Festival.
1923	Senior Prayer Meeting Topics, Poquonock Congregational Church, Rev. Victor L. Greenwood, Pastor.
1930	Tercentenary of the First Church, Windsor, Conn., 1630-1930. Windsor, Conn., B. S. Carter, 1930, 75p.
September 28, 1934	Poquonock Community Church, notice of Harvest Festival.

Record Books Not Printed

March 13, 1822 - April 1, 1822	Record in manuscript form, Poquonock Philosophical Debating Society.
Oct. 30, 1849	Library Book, Poquonock Library, established Jan. 24, 1828.
May 4, 1833 - May 7, 1835	Constitution and Records of the Poquonock Ladies Charitable Society.
July 26, 1841 - May 1857	Female Charitable Society, of 2nd Parish in Windsor, Treasurer's Book.
1841	Church Book, Poquonock Congregational Church.
Oct. 10, 1848 - Sept. 6, 1855	Universalist Ladies Sewing Society, sometimes called Universalist Ladies Society Record of meetings.
Oct. 10, 1849 - Oct. 20, 1887	Universalist Ladies Society Treasurer's Record.

Poquonock Congregational Society connected with the 2nd Church, Windsor better known of as the Poquonock Congregational Church.

Ladies Benevolent Society, Poquonock, Treasurer's Book.

Poquonock Sabbath School Records, names, attendance, number of Bible verses learned, collection.

57   Secretary's Book Good Samaritan Society of Poquonock, Conn.

- 1890 Report of the Ladies' Benevolent Society, Poquonock, Conn.

Sunday School Attendance

1899   Missionary Society Auxilliary to the Woman's Home Missionary Union of Conn.

Poquonock Sunday School Record for Librarian,

Total Abscience Benevolence.

1902   Good Citizenship Club, Secretary and Treasurer.

Young People's Society Christian Education.

Woman's Missionary Society Foreign Section.

Ladies Benevolent Society.

Poquonock Christian Endeavor Society membership list.

Poquonock Missionary S o c i e t y, Treasurer's Book.

Christian   Endeavor   Treasurer's Book.

Ladies Benevolent Society.

L a d i e s Benevolent Society, Poquonock Community Church.

Minutes Young People's Society.

Libraries and Denominational Headquarters

Andover-Newton Theological Institution, Newton Center, Mass.

Baker Memorial Library	Dartmouth College, Hanover, N. H.
Bangor Theological Seminary Library	Bangor, Maine
Case Memorial Library	Hartford Seminary Foundation.
Hartford Public Library	Hartford, Conn.
New Haven Colonial Historical Society	New Haven, Conn.
Union Theological Seminary	New York City, N. Y.
Watkinson Library	Hartford, Conn.
Williams College Library	Williamstown, Mass.
Windsor Public Library	Windsor, Conn.
Yale University Library	New Haven, Conn.
Congregational House	37 Garden Street Hartford, Conn.
Connecticut Baptist Convention	Hartford, Conn.
Universalist Head Quarters	Boston, Mass.

When Miss Charlotte Phelps Kendrick passed away January 15, 1955, she was Director of Religious Education, Center Congregational Church, Torrington, Connecticut. This appendix has been added by her mother, Mrs. Alexis D. Kendrick, c historian for the Poquonock Community Church Congregational, Inc. *18 Marshall. Phelps Rd. Windsor, Conn*

The account book kept by Rev. Daniel Foster and papers of the first three pastors of the Poquonock Church are in the Connecticut State Library. Rev. Foster received an honorary A.M. degree from Dartmouth College in 1774.

The Poquonock Community (Congregational) Church was dedicated April 12, 1854. The Parsonage including the land cost $1,500.00. Individual people erected sheds for their teams. Rev. Mr. Rouse was the first pastor to live in the Parsonage. All notices were put on the buttonball tree in front of the church. Ira Soper was tything master. One and three-eights acres of land was purchased for the church building.

During the pastorate of Rev. Mr. Lamb the barn was built and an addition put on the parsonage.

During the pastorate of Rev. Ogden Hall it was voted to place a bell in the tower.

During the pastorate of Rev. Mr. Bonney furnaces were installed in the church and the Home Missionary Society Aid discontinued.

During the pastorate of Rev. William H. Phipps the buttonball tree was cut down and notices were placed on the church door. Insurance on the church property for $10,000.00 was taken. "Mr. Phipps was an artist and painted pictures and sold them almost to the last."

During the pastorate of Rev. Mr. Ketchum paper and clapboards were put on the parsonage and it was painted.

Samuel Rose who was tutored by Rev. Mr. Ketchum is the father of Rev. Dr. Philip M. Rose. In the Granite Monthly, February 1881 is a picture of Rev. Mr. Ketchum and a ten page article about him with specific reference to the Poquonock church.

During Rev. William H. Howard's pastorate it was voted to lower the pulpit.

During the pastorate of Rev. Mr. Pettibone the church was painted and the stained glass windows put in and a porch was put on the parsonage.

During the pastorate of Rev. Mr. Merwin the 50th anniversary of the church was observed.

During the church service July 6, 1902, the Individual Communion Service was used for the first time. It was given by Prof. and Mrs. Brackett of Hartford in memory of their daughter Mrs. William C. Prentiss.

During Rev. Mr. Grisbrook's pastorate a baptism font was given in memory of Jasper Lord by his brother and sister.

The annual meeting of the Hartford Council of Congregational churches was held here Nov. 3, 1903. Nineteen of the twenty-one churches were represented.

The free seat system was adopted.

The growing spirit of tolerance and appreciation among the various religious groups in the community began during Rev. Mr. Merwin's pastorate.

May 6, 1935, there was a memorial service for Mrs. Carr.

As in other churches in the state special exercises were held commemorating the Tercentenary celebration of Connecticut. An historical address was given by the writer of this thesis and the sermon by Rev. Roscoe Nelson. Special music was rendered.

In February 1939, Rev. William A. Slater became pastor of the church. In his pastorate the annual carol sing with the Roman Catholic Church choir was initiated. Three new floors were put in the parsonage and during the war letters written to those in the service. A Study club was organized and on Sunday, June 8, 1941 the 100th anniversary of the founding of the church was observed.

Rev. Graham D. Child followed Mr. Slater in 1943. An oil burner furnace was installed in the church. The Richard Osborn steeple fund was orignated during this time and funds amounted to over $1000.00 in 1954.

Rev. Paul R. Donavan came to Poquonock in October 1947 and a Pilgrim Fellowship of church youth was organized.

In November 5, 1950 Rev. Robert K. Barrows was ordained. December 1952 saw the dedication of a new organ. Memorial Cross and Candlesticks were given by Mr. Barney Rapaport in memory of Walter L. Wolf and new signs were erected on the church grounds.

In August 15, 1953 Rev. Charles G. Campbell became the minister. A recognition service was held Sunday, November 8, 1953. During his pastorate the church observed the 100th anniversary of the dedication of the building, April 12, 1954. Five former pastors attended the celebration.

A pulpit Bible and a book in which all of the memorials will be recorded was given by the Peterson Family in memory of Mr. Fred Peterson.

A library in memory of Charlotte Phelps Kendrick, made possible by voluntary contributions, is under the supervision of the Board of Religious Education of the church.

Additional notes concerning the 2nd Meeting House supply ministers:

From Abiel Griswold's account book June 9, 1789 to 2nd Society of Windsor, Dr. to boarding ye Rev. Elam Potter from April 25 to the ninth of June by intervals in the whole three weeks   0 18 0

To keeping his horse two weeks from April 25 to May 9   0 4 0

                                        1 2 0

(Extract from a letter of Mrs. Alice Wheaton Welsh to Mrs. C. M. Kendrick, September 29, 1949.)

"I wish to express my appreciation for all you have done in furnishing material for my pageant. Also to Charlotte for loaning her thesis to me, for without it the pageant would have been an impossibility."

Mrs. Welsh wrote and directed a pageant for the 300th anniversary of Poquonock which was given in the Elementary School October 2, 1949 to an overflowing house. She included every group of people who have ever lived in our village from the Indians down to the Jamaicans and those from other islands who come here in the summer to work.

The pastors at St. Joseph's Church, Poquonock (after Rev. Joseph Healy):

Rev. James Roche
Rev. Timothy Byrne
Rev. John Weldon
Rev. Joseph Flanagan
Rev. Patrick Fitzmaurice, present paster
St. Joseph's Dramatic Club is now St. Joseph's Guild.

At a meeting held November 10, 1936, the Spiritual Harmonical Society voted to give the real estate and property of the piritualist Society to the 2nd School Society of Windsor for the enefit of the Elm Grove Cemetery. The 2nd School Society sold e property known as Liberal Hall to the St. Casimir's Lithunian Society.

On October 4, 1956 the following records were placed in the tate Library at Hartford:

1 Vol. Poquonock Ladies Charitable Society 1833-1855
1 Vol. Universalist Ladies Sewing Society 1848-1887
1 folder miscellaneous papers 1727-1783

The miscellaneous papers concerning the first three ministers the first church in Poquonock are to be photostated.

The picture, Christ Going Through the Wheatfields, by Wehle as given to the church in loving memory of Annie M. Callenr by the 1915 Ocean Park Group.

STAINED GLASS WINDOWS 1888

South Side

Given by Stephen Griswold
Of Brooklyn, N. Y.
In memory of his mother
Lorinda Griswold

Given by Senaca Griswold
in memory of his mother
and sisters

Given by Richard D. Case

North Side

Given by
Mrs. Edgar A. Mosher
in memory of her husband

Given by
Mrs. Charles A. Hatheway
in memory of her husband

Given by
Mrs. Thomas K. Marcey
in memory of her parents
Mr. & Mrs. Amos Hatheway

Given by Lemuel R. Lord

Front

Fan-shaped window over the front door and two
vestibule windows given by Mr. Thomas Duncan
for the choir which was a male quartet.

In December 1956 Mrs. Dorothy Bailey of Northampton presented to the Poquonock Church, in memory of Genevieve Lord Berry, the silver service which once belonged to Mrs. Berry's mother, Mrs. Lemuel R. Lord.

At the present time Poquonock and Rainbow are predominately Roman Catholic. St. Joseph's Church has a beautiful edifice. At the present time they are making extensive renovations in the Church basement. Two new exits and kitchen equipment will be added in order that members of the parish might have a place to meet for some of the social activities.

Church attendance at the Protestant Church is increasing and the Sunday School is in need of more room. An Expansion Fund is in progress to build an addition and renovate the present sanctuary.

7002 010

Lightning Source UK Ltd.
Milton Keynes UK
UKHW021853121118
332198UK00006B/299/P